OUR FAMILY HOLIDAY ORGANIZER

Christmas is Coming

EMILIE BARNES

Illustrations by MICHAL SPARKS

HARVEST HOUSE PUBLISHERS

Eugene, Oregon 97402

Christmas Is Coming

Published by Harvest House Publishers
Eugene, Oregon 97402

ISBN 1-56507-912-4

Indigo Gate
1 Pegasus Drive
Colts Neck, NJ 07722
(732) 577-9333

Design and production by Garborg Design Works, Minneapolis, Minnesota

Printed in China.

98 99 00 01 02 03 04 05 06 07 / IM / 10 9 8 7 6 5 4 3 2 1

The
____
Family
Holiday Organizer

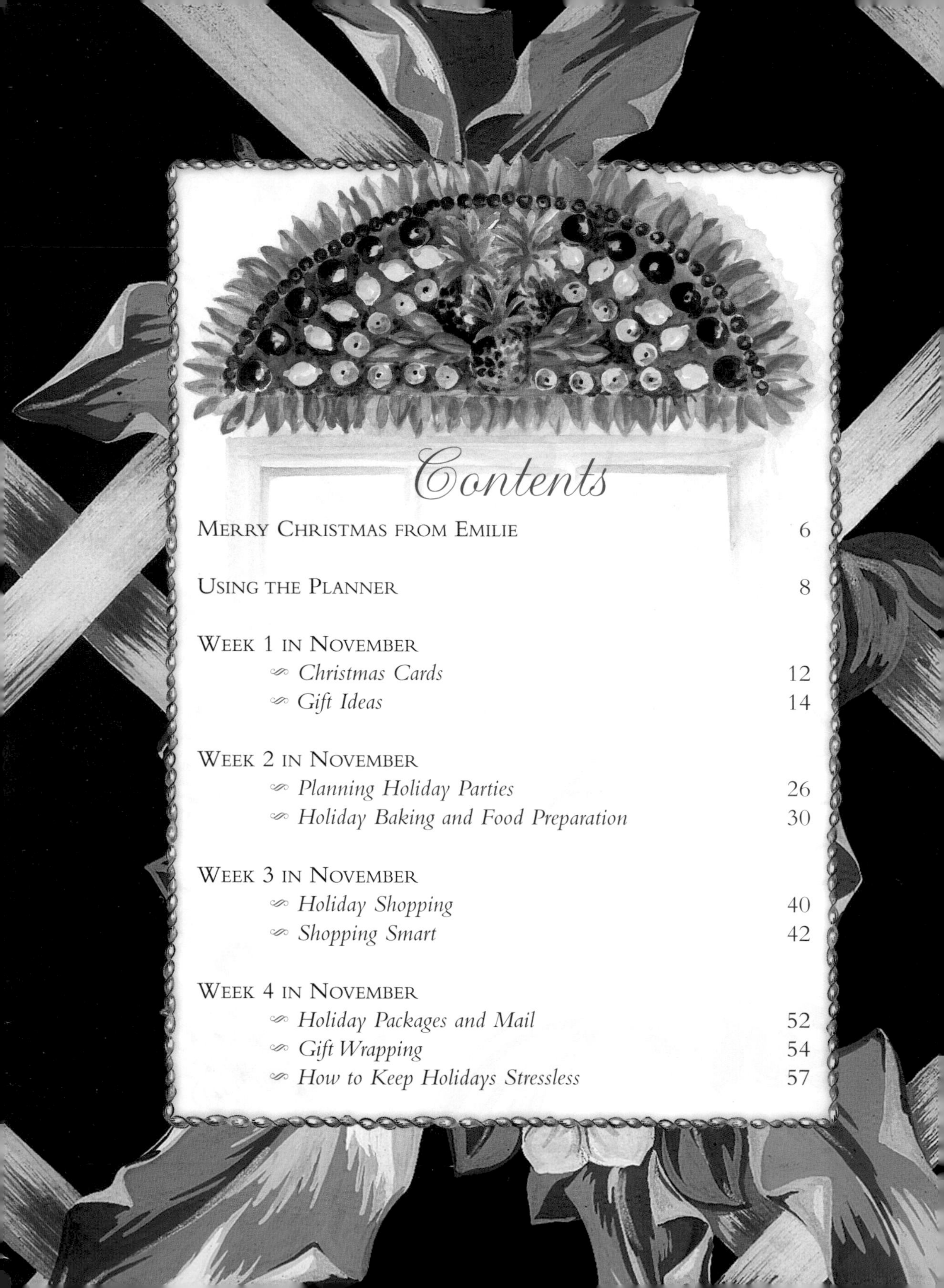

Contents

Christmas. It's my favorite time of year! I love having friends and family over, hearing favorite carols on the radio, and decorating the house in reds and greens, from top to bottom. It's that special time for giving…every present is carefully picked and wrapped (and hidden!). Rooftops sparkle with twinkling lights that decorate the whole neighborhood, and festive wreaths adorn front doors, heralding a celebration inside. We watch the Christmas pageant, and it's the "best one" ever. I love this season most of all for the joy that fills us, a joy that brings happiness and a desire to give of ourselves, for others.

So many activities to enjoy, and all of them occur in a few short weeks. Throughout the years, I've celebrated the season with special

trimmings, and my main goal during the hustle and bustle has always been the same—to enjoy Christmas!

I use a handy game plan to keep up with the details and fun that fill my winter calendar. (And this planner is designed to use for three years.) By planning ahead of time when I need to decorate, bake, shop, and write season's greetings, I enjoy the season so much more. I don't stress about trying to get everything done, because I know I *can* get everything done. The plan is realistic and sums up what is most important to me to get done for the season.

What I've learned I want to share with you, because it is my hope that this will be the best Christmas ever for you—one with plenty of time to enjoy family, friends, and the real meaning of the season.

Merry Christmas!

Emilie

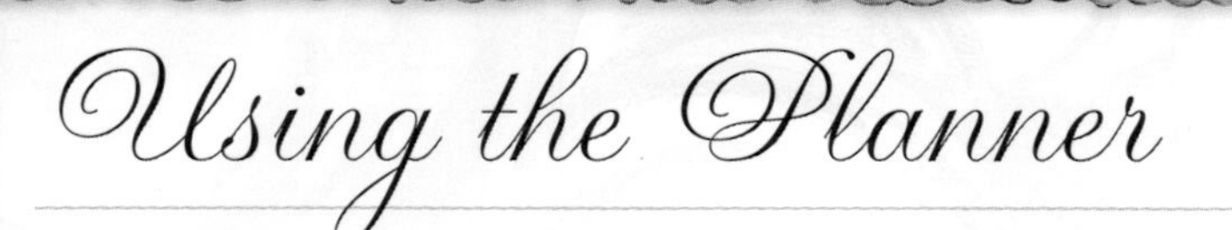

Using the Planner

Christmas was meant to be enjoyed, and by planning ahead, it's easy! Scheduling activities week by week lessens the last-minute rush to get everything done, making those activities the special expressions of Christmas we want them to be. Use this planner for three years (there is a place to note the year), and you'll find your Christmases calmer, more fun, and joyous.

A "To Do List" plans activities for each week with extra space for personal additions. Use the big shopping list to record all the errands, groceries, and gifts to buy—everything is in one convenient place! And the calendar works the list and activities into your weekly schedule so you know exactly what to expect each week.

MORE HANDY HELPS ARE IN THE BACK OF THE PLANNER:

∽ ***Christmas Card Record:*** Keep track of cards sent and received, along with everyone's current addresses.

∽ ***"Gifts Given" Record:*** Record all presents to be given at Christmas.

∽ ***"Gifts Received" List:*** Record all gifts received, who they are from, and when thank-you notes are completed.

∽ ***Shopping Guide:*** The perfect place to note sizes and preferences for everyone on your gift-giving list.

∽ ***"On Order" List:*** Keep track of your catalog orders so you'll know when to make follow-up phone calls.

∽ ***Hospitality Chart:*** Prepare holiday parties with a schedule to keep plans in order.

∽ ***Important Phone Numbers:*** Save names and phone numbers of that wonderful caterer, flowershop, or stationery store where you found great Christmas items.

November

WEEK 1

Christmas Cards

Nothing cheers my day like getting a note from an old friend. I love reading newsy letters and seeing photos of our friends and family. We collect all the holiday cards in a big basket and enjoy them the whole season.

A procrastinating Englishman named Henry Cole began the Christmas card tradition. In 1843, Cole was behind in his correspondence with friends and wanted to make everything right with a nice Christmas note to end the year. His resourceful idea led to a mass marketing of holiday cards, and the world has shared season's greetings ever since. Surprisingly, the first cards look much like those we see today, and the message remains the same: "A Merry Christmas and a Happy New Year."

Cards are personal selections; they reflect who we are and what we believe. Some are religious, some are humorous, but all of them express our love to those we care about. With rising postal costs and increasingly busy schedules, many people have geared down on

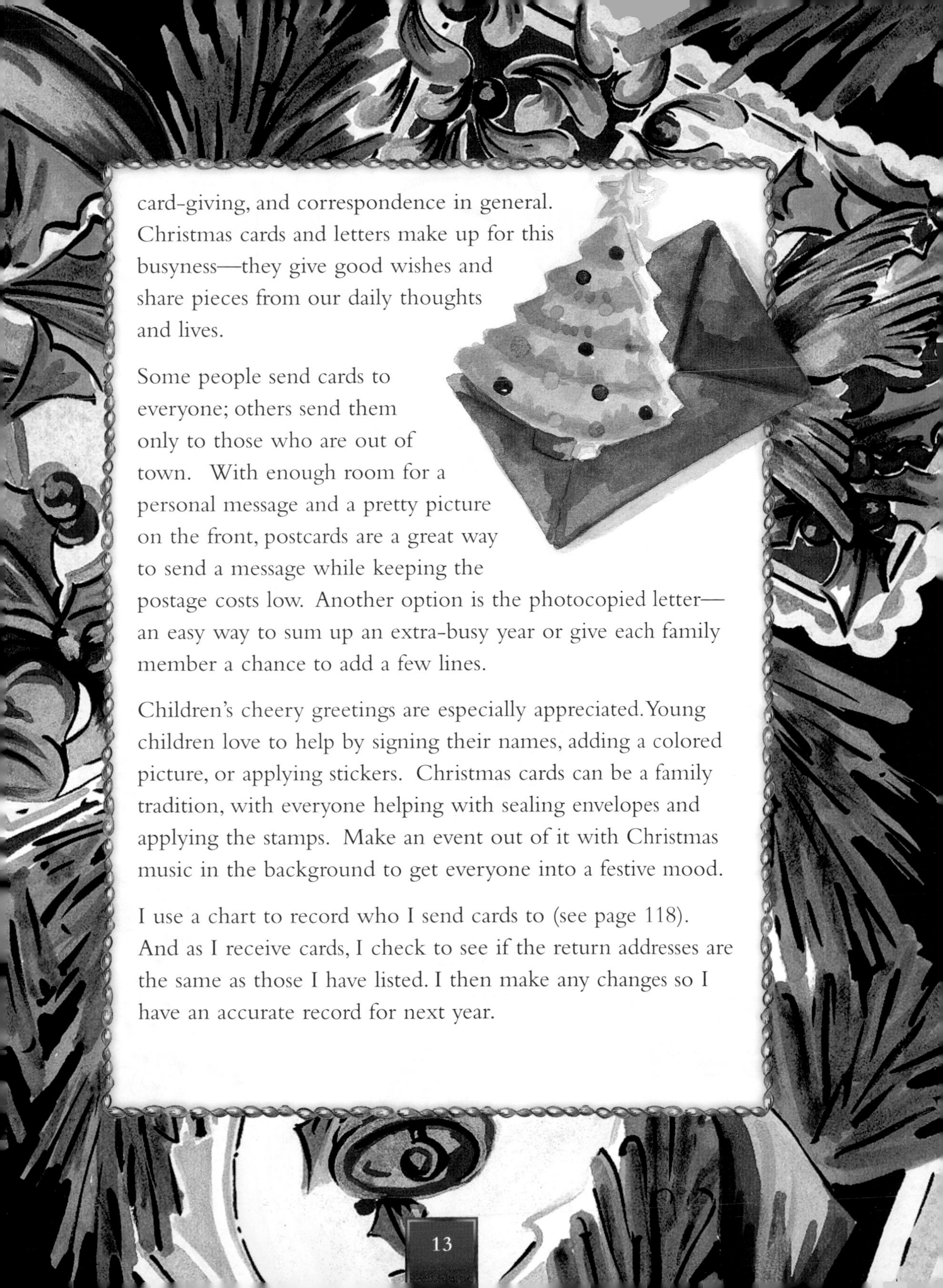

card-giving, and correspondence in general. Christmas cards and letters make up for this busyness—they give good wishes and share pieces from our daily thoughts and lives.

Some people send cards to everyone; others send them only to those who are out of town. With enough room for a personal message and a pretty picture on the front, postcards are a great way to send a message while keeping the postage costs low. Another option is the photocopied letter—an easy way to sum up an extra-busy year or give each family member a chance to add a few lines.

Children's cheery greetings are especially appreciated. Young children love to help by signing their names, adding a colored picture, or applying stickers. Christmas cards can be a family tradition, with everyone helping with sealing envelopes and applying the stamps. Make an event out of it with Christmas music in the background to get everyone into a festive mood.

I use a chart to record who I send cards to (see page 118). And as I receive cards, I check to see if the return addresses are the same as those I have listed. I then make any changes so I have an accurate record for next year.

Gift Ideas

Gifts can be whatever you want them to be, and everyone loves the special touch in a gift of your own creation. For unique, homemade, holiday wishes:

- Make a batch of bran muffins. You can give the recipe and six fresh muffins baked in the tin. With clear cellophane wrapped around the tin and a pretty bow on top, anyone who loves muffins will be delighted.

Emilie's Bran Muffins

Preheat oven to 350 degrees. Grease muffin pan or line with muffin papers.

Cover 1 cup raisins with warm water and let stand 5 to 10 minutes.

Blend together and let stand for 5 minutes:

½ cup boiling water
1½ cups unprocessed wheat bran

Blend together thoroughly with wire whisk in order given:

1 egg
¼ to ⅓ cup honey
1 cup buttermilk
bran mixture

Blend dry ingredients together in separate bowl:

1½ cups whole wheat or whole wheat pastry flour
1¼ teaspoons soda
1 teaspoon salt
1 cup chopped walnuts
1 cup chopped or diced dates
1 cup shredded coconut, unsweetened

Blend drained raisins, then dry ingredients into liquid ingredients just until mixed. Do not overmix! Fill muffin cups almost full. Fill any empty cups halfway with water. Bake 20 to 25 minutes. Cool 5 to 10 minutes before removing from pan.

- Give a favorite recipe, and with it include one or two ingredients. One of my favorites is a triple-chocolate-cake recipe. Everyone loves it, and it's so easy—only three steps and five minutes. I give a copy of the recipe, a package of chocolate chips, a box of chocolate pudding, and a box of chocolate cake mix.

Emilie's Triple Chocolate Fudge Cake

Prepare a 3⅜ ounce package of chocolate pudding mix (cooked type) as directed on package. Blend chocolate cake mix (dry mix) into hot pudding. Pour ingredients into greased and floured 13 x 9 inch pan. Sprinkle with ½ cup semisweet chocolate pieces and ½ cup chopped nuts. Bake 30 to 35 minutes at 350 degrees.
Serve warm with whipped cream or ice cream.

- Package in a Zip-Lock bag a mixture of dry beans and include a favorite bean soup recipe. This is a great idea for large families. Delicious! I make enough soup mix for eight bags with 2½ cups of beans for each gift:

Combine the following in a large container:

2 cups black beans	2 cups butter beans or large limas
2 cups pinto beans	2 cups navy beans
2 cups pearl barley	2 cups split green peas
2 cups small lima beans	2 cups red beans
2 cups lentils	2 cups Great Northern Beans

Yummy Bean Soup

1 package of gift beans
1 large onion, chopped
1 29-ounce can tomatoes
1 clove crushed garlic
juice of 1 lemon
salt and pepper to taste

Wash beans thoroughly and place in large pot. Add enough water to cover beans by two inches. Boil two minutes and let stand one hour. Drain and add two quarts of water and ½ pound of ham or ham hocks and simmer 1½ to 2 hours, covered. Add the rest of the ingredients and simmer 30 minutes or until beans are tender. Makes 10 to 12 big servings.

- Cover shoe boxes with wrapping paper, wallpaper, contact paper, etc., and use as a gift box. Fill with stationery items—glue stick, small scissors, paper clips, marking pens, memo pad, and thank-you notes. Any mom, dad, grandparent, or teacher would love such a gift.

- Cover a box with road maps and fill the box with more road maps, a first-aid kit, a teaching tape or your favorite music tape, jumper cables, flares, or any kind of item associated with travel or a car.
- Take baby food jars and apply cute stickers to the front. Three of these make a great gift for storing cotton balls, bath salts, Q-tips, etc.
- Baskets make great gifts filled with items:

  Bath—soaps, shower cap, bubble bath, bath oil, washcloth
  Reading—book for each family member, bookmarks
  Kitchen—wooden spoons, measuring cups, can opener, etc.
  Toys—games, books, teddy bear, dolls, truck, puzzles, etc.
  Grandma—bib to use for grandbabies, toy, rattle, book of short stories, baby items, etc.
  Gardening—seeds, garden tools, gloves, pruners/clippers, hand shovel, fertilizer, potted plants
  Sewing—measuring tape, scissors, pins, jars of buttons, elastic lace, ribbon, tape, etc.
  Laundry—bleach, laundry powder or liquid, fabric softener, spray spot remover, small spot brush
  For men—car wax, chamois, Armor-all, trash bags, litter bag for car

- Food items always make great gifts. Items that are uniquely part of your area or hometown are sure to be special to friends and family. Every year we receive a bag of raw peanuts; it's one of our favorite gifts. Here are more food ideas:

  Popcorn
  Breads—banana, zucchini, pumpkin
  Nuts—almonds, walnuts
  Caramel corn
  Pure natural maple syrup
  Fresh fruits are a great gift. Our orange trees provide a steady supply for friends who aren't in sunny climates. Avocados and dried fruits are also good. Baskets of natural foods such as

granola mix, raisins, and three-to-seven-grain cereal mix are great gifts for those who are health-conscious.

Santa Claus and Gift Giving

Many people do not know that there is a special story about who Santa Claus really was. There was a dear Christian man who lived a long time ago. His name was Nicholas, and we call him St. Nicholas. In his town there were many poor children; they didn't have enough food, clothes, or toys. St. Nicholas used his money to buy them what they needed. He didn't want them to be embarrassed by his gifts, so he gave them secretly.

St. Nick always gave in the spirit of helping and sharing, and we follow his example when we celebrate gift-giving. All the gifts he gave and all of the gifts we give remind us that it's better to give than to receive.

- Give gifts to all your neighbors. A cookie baking day with your children, grandchildren, or Sunday school class is a wonderful time to grow closer and give them a little experience in the kitchen. Bake and decorate cookies, then place them on colorful paper plates and wrap them in clear cellophane wrap. A festive ribbon or bow is all the cookies need to be a wonderful surprise for neighbors. And delivering them personally is a wonderful chance to visit elderly people and neighbors you don't always see.
- Another fun idea is to give a dated ornament each year. Take the time to find the perfect ornament to reflect that special someone's interests or personality. Write the year on the back of the ornament to make it a special keepsake. Many of our tree trimmings go back 15 to 20 years in time, and it's so special to see when they became part of the tradition at our home.

When visiting friends during the holidays, stealthily slip an ornament on their tree. Attach a small gift tag if you would like. When they are taking down their tree, it will be a nice post-Christmas surprise.

Remember, it's the thought that counts! Be creative and there's no end to what can be made into a gift.

As Christmas approached, the usual mysteries began to haunt the house...

LOUISA MAY ALCOTT, *Little Women*

YEAR _____

November

WEEK 1

TO DO LIST

- Make a list of people to receive Christmas cards
- Purchase cards
- Stock up on baking supplies
- Begin gift-giving list of who to buy for

Weekly Calendar

Sunday

Monday

Tuesday

Wednesday

Thursday

Friday

Saturday

Shopping List

Tip of the Week

Set up a Christmas card station in the living room, and have the whole family help with the sealing, stamping, and addressing.

May the light of Christmastide shed its cheering ray o'er thy homestead and abide with thee every day.

E.A.L. KNIGHT

YEAR _____

November

WEEK 1

TO DO LIST

- Make a list of people to receive Christmas cards
- Purchase cards
- Stock up on baking supplies
- Begin gift-giving list of who to buy for

Weekly Calendar

Sunday

Monday

Tuesday

Wednesday

Thursday

Friday

Saturday

Shopping List

Tip of the Week

Spray your holiday tablecloths with a fabric protector. Spills will be easier to remove.

Heap the holly! Wreath the pine!
Train the dainty Christmas vine~
Let the breadth of fir and bay
Mingle on the festal day.

HELEN CHASE

YEAR _____

November

WEEK 1

TO DO LIST

- Make a list of people to receive Christmas cards
- Purchase cards
- Stock up on baking supplies
- Begin gift-giving list of who to buy for

Weekly Calendar

Sunday

Monday

Tuesday

Wednesday

Thursday

Friday

Saturday

Shopping List

Tip of the Week

The selection of your Christmas cards can be made early in November. But the best way is to have purchased your cards at 50 percent off right after the previous Christmas.

November

WEEK 2

Planning Holiday Parties

Parties are such a wonderful way to see friends and celebrate the season. And because everyone is so busy attending these fun events, planning ahead is a must. I usually send out invitations for my Christmas tea and open house in the last week of November. People make their plans around the invitations that come first, so I know mine will be received early enough to give my friends time to schedule it in.

By the second week of December, I have the menu planned and I'm ready to shop for ingredients. It works well to shop for the Christmas Eve goodies and Christmas breakfast brunch menu at the same time. One trip through the grocery store will get everything I need for parties so I can concentrate on baking and freezing whatever can be done ahead.

Holiday Wassail Recipe

Try this delicious recipe for wassail! Your house will smell wonderful, and friends and family will love it!

1 gallon apple cider
1 large can pineapple juice (unsweetened)
¾ cup strong tea (herbal tea optional)
Place in a cheesecloth sack:
1 tablespoon whole cloves
1 tablespoon whole allspice
2 sticks cinnamon

Place all in a crockpot or on the stove. Let it simmer slowly for four to six hours. Add water if it evaporates too much. Yum!

Table Settings for the Party

The table and centerpiece are the big decoration for a party; they set off the wonderful food and punch that everyone loves. I have fun mixing and matching my table settings. To make the decorations creative and different, I use sheets to make the tablecloths and napkins. I'll take the saucer from my set of eight dishes to the store to look for sheets that might match or coordinate. Many times I'll find a sheet on sale that will work perfectly. I keep my eyes open all year for the perfect addition to my holiday decorating.

To make one tablecloth and 12 napkins for a standard-size table, use a king-size flat

I use a hospitality chart (see page 136) to write down my schedule and menu in one place:

Schedule

Last Week of November
- Send out invitations

First Week of December
- Plan centerpiece, order if necessary
- Prepare menu
- Make shopping list

Second Week of December
- Shop for ingredients, decorations
- Bake/prepare anything that can be frozen
- Check RSVP list for number of guests

Three Days Before
- Polish silver
- Clean house as needed
- Grate cheese, chop nuts, prepare garnishes
- Review menu, make sure all ingredients are present

One Day Before
- Clean and prep vegetables, make trays
- Defrost appetizers, goodies
- Set table, place centerpiece, candles, and other decorations
- Cook main course and any hot dishes or last-minute items
- Clean and touch up the house

Day of Party
- Make punch or wassail
- Make trays of appetizers, goodies
- Warm up hot appetizers, main courses

Last Minute
- Put out relishes, cranberry sauce, or condiments
- Have a wonderful time!

Menu

Appetizers

sesame seed chicken wings
angel food cake with fondue
brie and apples

Entree

roasted turkey

Side Dish

baked holiday tomatoes

Salad

red jello fruit salad
veggie medley

Dessert

chocolate pecan mousse
cookie tray

Beverages

holiday wassail
raspberry punch
coffee

sheet. If you don't want so many napkins, or if you have a small table, you can use a full- or queen-size sheet. Leave the sheet's border on and there's less to hem. To find the right size, measure the length and width of your table and add 6" to hang over each side. Then add one inch for a turn-under hem. Cut your tablecloth out first.

Then make your napkins out of the remainder. I like big napkins, so mine are 18" square, but you may want a smaller napkin. One yard of fabric will yield six 15" square napkins. And it's always nice to finish the napkins with lace or eyelet embroidery.

If you are making a round tablecloth, fold the sheet in half and cut a string the length of the radius of your table plus a six-inch drop and one-inch hem. I mark my half-circle cutting lines with pins, but chalk works too.

FOLD

Another option is to buy holiday fabric such as taffeta, felt, or even lace panel curtains. A green or red felt fabric tablecloth is great for Christmas. It doesn't have to be hemmed, and it's nice and wide so no sewing is needed. Also, today's new felt is completely washable. It looks beautiful as it is, or you can add a plaid runner, taffeta overcloth, or holiday place mats to dress it up.

Napkin Rings

I use napkin rings to set off a pretty table and tie the colors all together. If I have a green, red, and gold plaid tablecloth and solid red napkins, I tie it together with gold-painted napkin rings. Any combination is possible, and it's easy to be creative!

For fast napkin rings, cover empty toilet paper rolls with lace and cut the rolls 2" or 3" in width.

Cookie cutters (plastic or metal) make great napkin rings. You can find them in gourmet stores, kitchen sections of department stores, and catalogs. They come in all shapes.

I have also used napkin rings to hold special wishes for guests. Take your paper towel tube and cut it in 2" widths. Then cut each ring so it opens. Write a Scripture or blessing inside, and, with your glue gun or regular glue, cover the outside with ribbon, leaving tails long enough on each side of the opening to tie a bow. Slide your napkin through the ring. When family members or guests untie the bow, have them read the message.

One year we were having 26 people over for Christmas dinner. I was using an old standby poinsettia fabric tablecloth I had used previously, but I wanted to jazz it up a bit. I found some wooden napkin rings—cheap! I bought some red silk poinsettia flowers (small version), cut off the long stems, and glue-gunned the flowers to the plain wooden rings. It was sensational with my green napkins, and I've used them for the past four years. They store well and keep their shape wonderfully.

Centerpieces

Centerpieces can be made out of whatever you have. I've made arrangements with dried flowers, candles, teacups, ornaments, and even my nativity scene. Centerpieces can highlight the theme of a party, the food being served, or just whatever you happen to like.

A group of candles (6 to 10) of different heights makes a beautiful focal point, and they keep the decorating simple yet elegant. Tie a plaid Christmas bow around the base of your candles or around the candle holder itself. You can change the ribbons and bows to celebrate each season or holiday.

Scooped-out apples are a great place to put votive candles. This makes a unique centerpiece. Squeeze lemon juice on the apple's insides so it doesn't turn brown. The apples will last for about a week.

A wreath set on a glass plate with candles in the center is also pretty on the table. Pine cones, poinsettias, flowers, ribbon, moss, ivy, and holly are all great additions to the wreath if you need to dress it up a little.

Potted poinsettia plants or silk poinsettia flowers in a pretty basket are a lovely centerpiece. Stuff moss around the top of the basket to cover the plastic pot, and add ribbons and bows to make it festive.

The Candy Cane

Legend says the candy cane was invented by a Christian in England in the seventeenth century. At that time, the government would not let people celebrate Christmas. So, a candy maker made candy shaped like a shepherd's crook to be a secret symbol of Jesus. The white stripe represented the purity of Jesus and the red stripe represented His life that He gave for each of us. The candy was a double gift: a sweet treat and a symbol of Christmas.

Holiday Baking and Food Preparation

Christmas goodies and sweets are what our tastebuds enjoy during the season. And since baked goods freeze beautifully, I like to start early. My family likes this schedule because the house smells so wonderful and they can start eating them that much sooner. I usually bake rolls, breads, cookies and even a few desserts that stand freezing well at this point. And I add to the freezer whenever I have an extra afternoon or evening. My children enjoyed helping with this task because it was an opportunity to talk, listen to Christmas music, and be together. They looked forward to filling the freezer almost as much as I did!

Peppermint Candy Cane Cookies

- 1 cup sugar
- 1 cup butter
- ½ cup milk
- 1 egg
- 1 teaspoon salt
- 1 teaspoon peppermint extract
- 3½ cups all-purpose flour
- 1 teaspoon baking powder
- ¼ teaspoon salt
- ½ teaspoon red food coloring

Mix sugar, butter, milk, egg, and vanilla. Add peppermint. Stir in flour, baking powder, and salt. Divide dough into halves, tint 1 half with red food coloring. Cover and refrigerate at least 4 hours.

Heat oven to 350 degrees. Roll ropes of each color of dough on floured surface and spiral one of each color together for candy cane effect. After placing it on the cookie sheet, curve the top of the cookie to form the handle of the cane. Bake until set and very light brown, 9 to 12 minutes. After baking, immediately sprinkle cookies with a mixture of 2 tablespoons crushed peppermint candy and 2 tablespoons sugar.

I always spend at least one day baking with my grandchildren. They help with the cut-outs and gingerbread men. I plan a day on the calendar just for this event, and when it comes, I have all the powdered sugar, sprinkles, candies, and food coloring I need. They love this tradition, and they are always so proud of their creations!

I bake fruitcakes, plum puddings, and anything else which needs time to mellow in the first week of December. Once that's done my freezer is bulging with Christmas goodies, and I'm relaxed knowing I have a good start on the holiday.

Now all our neighbors' chimneys smoke,
And Christmas logs are burning;
Their ovens with baked meats do choke,
And all their spits are turning.
Without the door let sorrow lie,
And if for cold it hap to die,
We'll bury it in Christmas pie,
And evermore be merry!

GEORGE WITHER

And there were shepherds living out in the fields nearby, keeping watch over their flocks at night.

THE BOOK OF LUKE

YEAR _____

November

WEEK 2

TO DO LIST

- Write Christmas cards
- Review budget for gift-giving
- Begin holiday baking
- Mark days for baking with your children on the calendar

Weekly Calendar

Sunday

Monday

Tuesday

Wednesday

Thursday

Friday

Saturday

Shopping List

Tip of the Week

If you cover dried fruits or nuts with flour before adding them to the batter, they won't sink to the bottom during baking.

It is good to be children sometimes,
and never better than at Christmas.

CHARLES DICKENS

YEAR _____

November

WEEK 2

TO DO LIST

- Write Christmas cards
- Review budget for gift-giving
- Begin holiday baking
- Mark days for baking with your children on the calendar

Weekly Calendar

Sunday

Monday

Tuesday

Wednesday

Thursday

Friday

Saturday

Shopping List

Tip of the Week

Christmas music is the best mood setter for a holiday party! Borrow from friends to have some variety throughout the event.

The best ornament of a dining room
is a well~cooked dinner.

MRS. HAWEIS

YEAR _____

November

WEEK 2

TO DO LIST

- Write Christmas cards
- Review budget for gift-giving
- Begin holiday baking
- Mark days for baking with your children on the calendar

Weekly Calendar

Sunday

Monday

Tuesday

Wednesday

Thursday

Friday

Saturday

Shopping List

Tip of the Week

Add some fun to a holiday dinner party with a gingerbread man propped by each person's water glass and a nametag around each cookie's neck.

November

WEEK

3

Holiday Shopping

I love giving presents to everyone. I try and give a little something to anyone who has helped me throughout the year—from our paper boy to the not-so-often-seen dentist! They are all people who have given something to me, and I love to share my thanks with a surprise.

It's helpful to have a master list to chart the progress in this department. Otherwise I forget who I've bought for and who is left. The "Gifts Given" Record at the end of this book (see page 126) is great for keeping everything straight. I write down my homemade gifts and baskets too.

I ask my family to make wish lists for Christmas in November, and they are quite happy to help me. With their input, I have all sorts of ideas in mind by the last week of November. I love having time to mull over gift ideas before I begin shopping. My shopping trips are more efficient because I'm not so tempted to buy impulsively when I have thought through each person's gift.

I usually finish my shopping by the second week of December, and then I focus on homemade gifts and baskets the following week. (The second week of December is a good time to check on catalog orders too. Use the "On Order" List on page 134 to help you keep track of catalog orders. Shop for necessary gift substitutes or have Plan B ready if the order doesn't arrive in time.)

Shopping Smart

1. Make a list based on the shops within a particular mall. Work your way around mentally, jotting down specific people you need to find gifts for. Decide before you go out if this year you are purchasing "one big gift" or lots of little things.

2. Write down what stores you need to go to, hopefully a majority of your shopping can be accomplished in one trip.

3. Take advantage of wrapping services and/or gift boxes, ribbon, and tissue. Have as many gifts as you can ready to place under the tree when you arrive home.

4. Do two things at once. If, for example, you purchase clothing for three people which includes gift-wrapping, allow the clerks to finish the packages while you visit other shops. Circle back at the end of the day and collect your packages.

5. For the hard-to-please people who have everything, a gift certificate to a restaurant, ice cream shop, or fast-food restaurant (children love that) is always a hit.

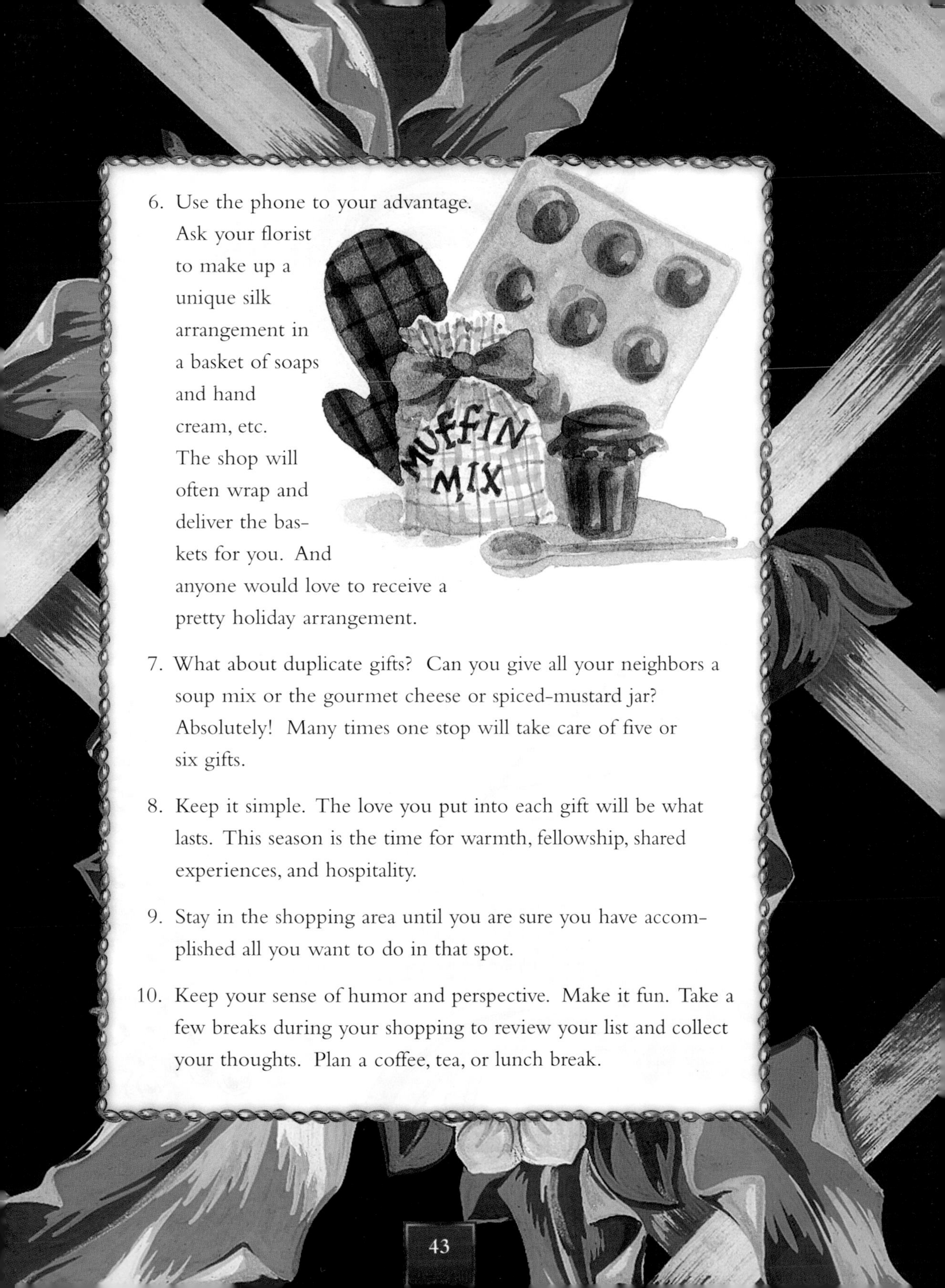

6. Use the phone to your advantage. Ask your florist to make up a unique silk arrangement in a basket of soaps and hand cream, etc. The shop will often wrap and deliver the baskets for you. And anyone would love to receive a pretty holiday arrangement.

7. What about duplicate gifts? Can you give all your neighbors a soup mix or the gourmet cheese or spiced-mustard jar? Absolutely! Many times one stop will take care of five or six gifts.

8. Keep it simple. The love you put into each gift will be what lasts. This season is the time for warmth, fellowship, shared experiences, and hospitality.

9. Stay in the shopping area until you are sure you have accomplished all you want to do in that spot.

10. Keep your sense of humor and perspective. Make it fun. Take a few breaks during your shopping to review your list and collect your thoughts. Plan a coffee, tea, or lunch break.

Blessed by the Christmas sunshine, our natures, perhaps long leaf-less, bring forth new love, new kindness, new mercy, new compassion.

HELEN KELLER

YEAR _____

November

WEEK 3

TO DO LIST

- Ask for family wish-lists
- Decide what kind of Christmas party to have, buy invitations
- Continue to bake goodies and freeze them

Weekly Calendar

Sunday

Monday | Tuesday

Wednesday | Thursday

Friday | Saturday

Shopping List

Tip of the Week

Children will love this Christmas gift idea: roll up a dollar bill and insert it into a balloon. Mail it along in a card with instructions to blow it up and then pop it.

It was the policy of the good old gentleman to make his children feel that home was the happiest place in the world; and I value this delicious home~feeling as one of the choicest gifts a parent can bestow.

WASHINGTON IRVING

YEAR _____

November

WEEK 3

TO DO LIST

- Ask for family wish-lists
- Decide what kind of Christmas party to have, buy invitations
- Continue to bake goodies and freeze them

Weekly Calendar

Sunday

Monday

Tuesday

Wednesday

Thursday

Friday

Saturday

Shopping List

Tip of the Week

A gift certificate for free babysitting or a homemade meal are great gifts for friends who seem to have everything!

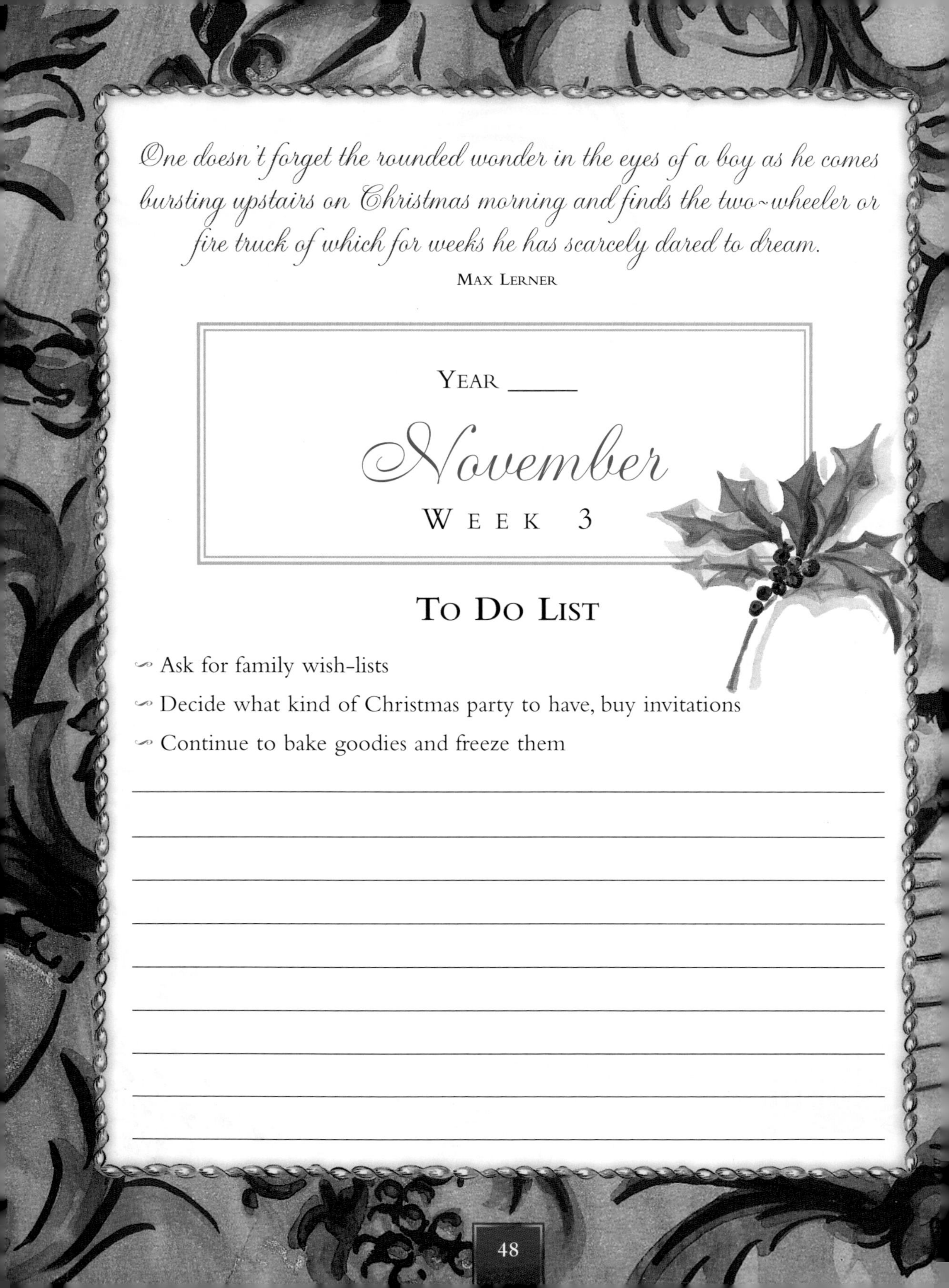

One doesn't forget the rounded wonder in the eyes of a boy as he comes bursting upstairs on Christmas morning and finds the two-wheeler or fire truck of which for weeks he has scarcely dared to dream.

MAX LERNER

YEAR _____

November

WEEK 3

TO DO LIST

- Ask for family wish-lists
- Decide what kind of Christmas party to have, buy invitations
- Continue to bake goodies and freeze them

Weekly Calendar

Sunday

Monday

Tuesday

Wednesday

Thursday

Friday

Saturday

Shopping List

Tip of the Week

A fresh bouquet of beautiful flowers wrapped in cellophane and tied with a big bow is one of my favorite gifts for friends who love plants and are longing for springtime.

November

WEEK 4

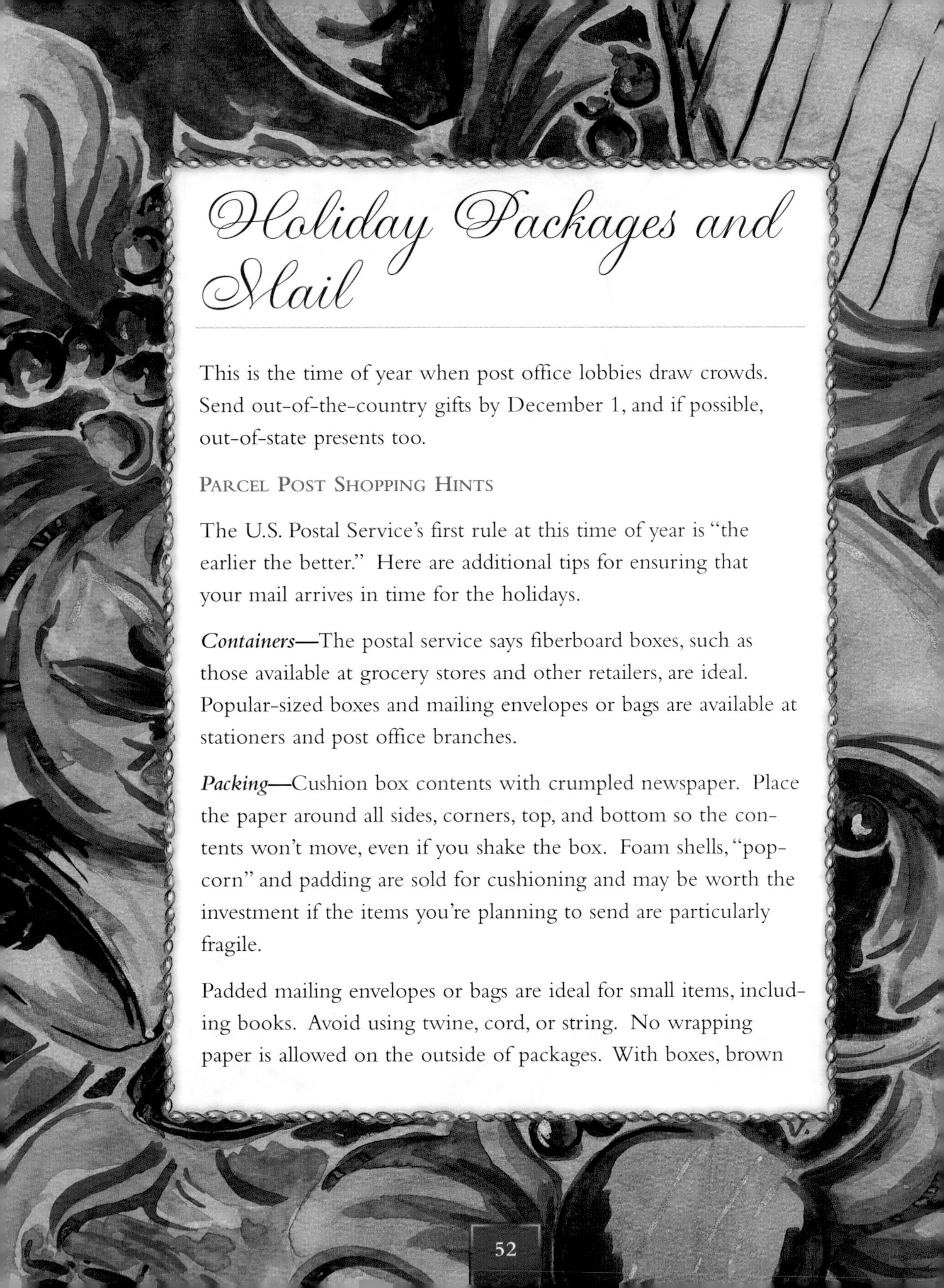

Holiday Packages and Mail

This is the time of year when post office lobbies draw crowds. Send out-of-the-country gifts by December 1, and if possible, out-of-state presents too.

PARCEL POST SHOPPING HINTS

The U.S. Postal Service's first rule at this time of year is "the earlier the better." Here are additional tips for ensuring that your mail arrives in time for the holidays.

***Containers*—**The postal service says fiberboard boxes, such as those available at grocery stores and other retailers, are ideal. Popular-sized boxes and mailing envelopes or bags are available at stationers and post office branches.

***Packing*—**Cushion box contents with crumpled newspaper. Place the paper around all sides, corners, top, and bottom so the contents won't move, even if you shake the box. Foam shells, "popcorn" and padding are sold for cushioning and may be worth the investment if the items you're planning to send are particularly fragile.

Padded mailing envelopes or bags are ideal for small items, including books. Avoid using twine, cord, or string. No wrapping paper is allowed on the outside of packages. With boxes, brown

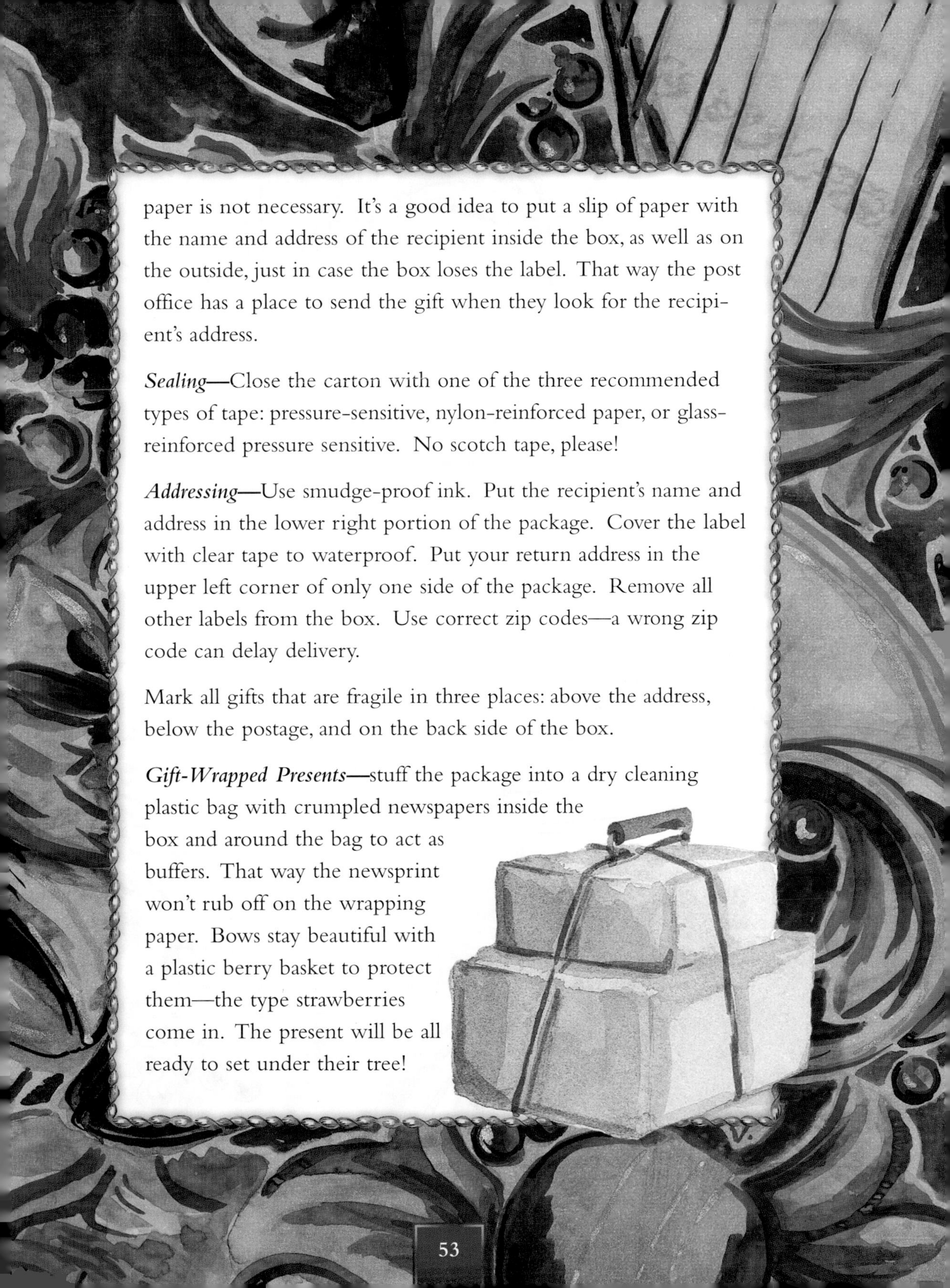

paper is not necessary. It's a good idea to put a slip of paper with the name and address of the recipient inside the box, as well as on the outside, just in case the box loses the label. That way the post office has a place to send the gift when they look for the recipient's address.

Sealing—Close the carton with one of the three recommended types of tape: pressure-sensitive, nylon-reinforced paper, or glass-reinforced pressure sensitive. No scotch tape, please!

Addressing—Use smudge-proof ink. Put the recipient's name and address in the lower right portion of the package. Cover the label with clear tape to waterproof. Put your return address in the upper left corner of only one side of the package. Remove all other labels from the box. Use correct zip codes—a wrong zip code can delay delivery.

Mark all gifts that are fragile in three places: above the address, below the postage, and on the back side of the box.

Gift-Wrapped Presents—stuff the package into a dry cleaning plastic bag with crumpled newspapers inside the box and around the bag to act as buffers. That way the newsprint won't rub off on the wrapping paper. Bows stay beautiful with a plastic berry basket to protect them—the type strawberries come in. The present will be all ready to set under their tree!

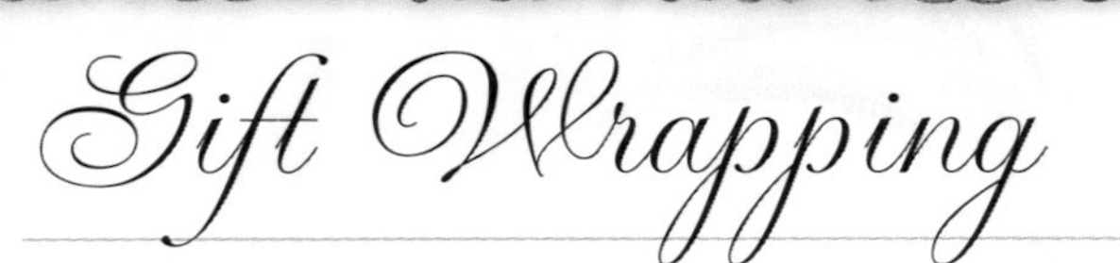

Gift Wrapping

I like to buy Christmas gift wrap right after Christmas when everything is on sale, but November is a great time to restock scotch tape, gift tags, red, green, and white ribbon, and tissue paper. That way you have it on hand for quick wrapping.

The Perfect Giftwrap Center

I have a holiday gift wrapping station, and I love having everything in one place. I find all sorts of wrapping possibilities because I add to my giftwrap center all year. Here's what a station can include:

- Scissors
- Tape, double-stick for packages
- Mailing tape, filament reinforced
- Wrapping paper
- White craft paper and rubber stamps to decorate it
- Cellophane, clear
- Ribbons
- Tags or enclosure cards
- Gift boxes
- Gift bags and totes
- Tissue paper
- Newspapers—comics, sports page, stockmarket
- Fabrics

Being creative with gift wrap is easy and can be inexpensive—like using newsprint to wrap dad's gift. The stock market, sports, travel, comic, or business section with Christmas ribbon is an easy and original wrapping treatment.

I like to wrap cookbooks and kitchen items in a tea towel. If it's an educational book, use road maps as the paper. A hand-sewn gift looks great with a measuring tape for a bow. Leftover lace pieces and rickrack are great for little additions.

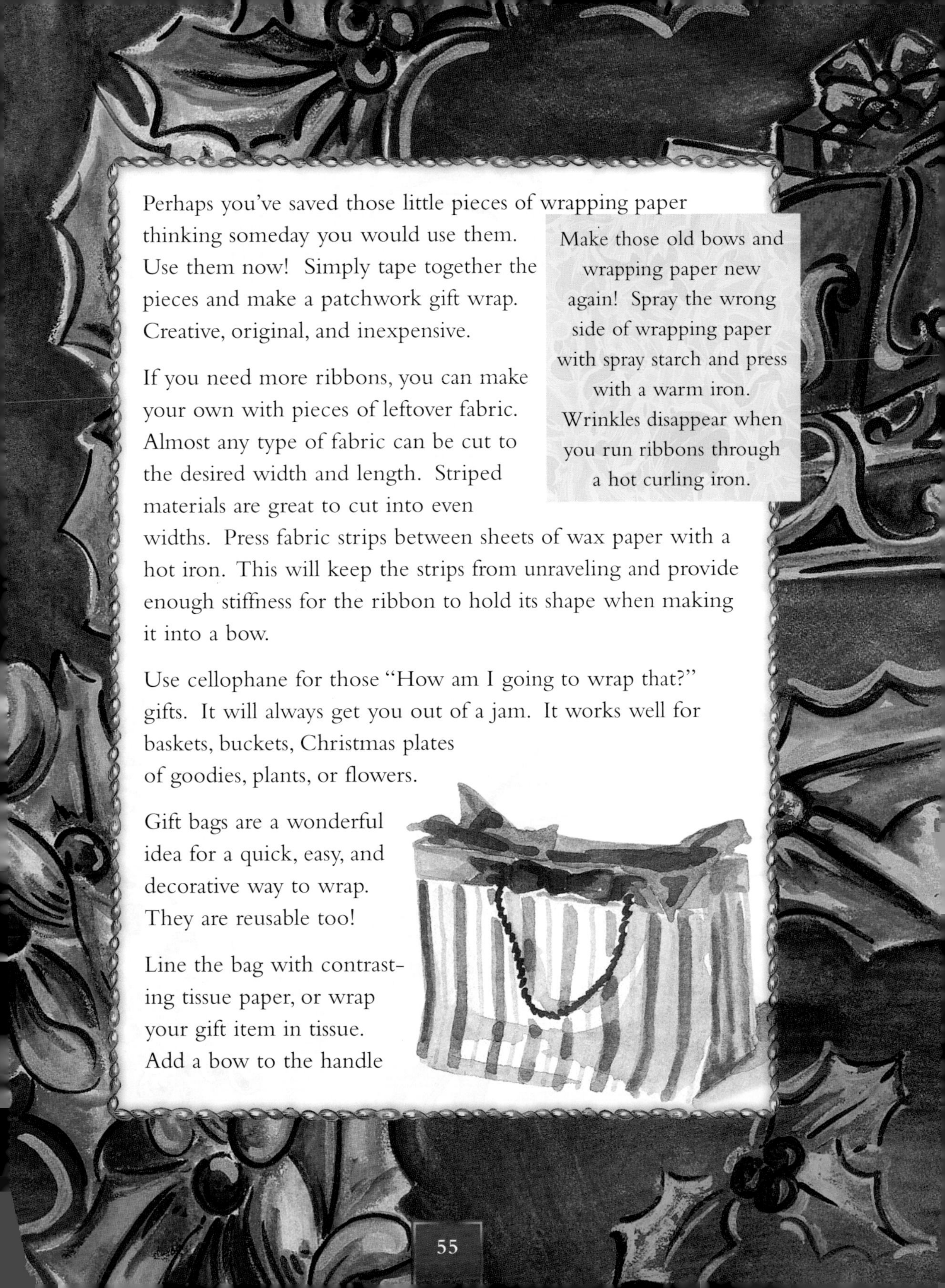

Perhaps you've saved those little pieces of wrapping paper thinking someday you would use them. Use them now! Simply tape together the pieces and make a patchwork gift wrap. Creative, original, and inexpensive.

Make those old bows and wrapping paper new again! Spray the wrong side of wrapping paper with spray starch and press with a warm iron. Wrinkles disappear when you run ribbons through a hot curling iron.

If you need more ribbons, you can make your own with pieces of leftover fabric. Almost any type of fabric can be cut to the desired width and length. Striped materials are great to cut into even widths. Press fabric strips between sheets of wax paper with a hot iron. This will keep the strips from unraveling and provide enough stiffness for the ribbon to hold its shape when making it into a bow.

Use cellophane for those "How am I going to wrap that?" gifts. It will always get you out of a jam. It works well for baskets, buckets, Christmas plates of goodies, plants, or flowers.

Gift bags are a wonderful idea for a quick, easy, and decorative way to wrap. They are reusable too!

Line the bag with contrasting tissue paper, or wrap your gift item in tissue. Add a bow to the handle

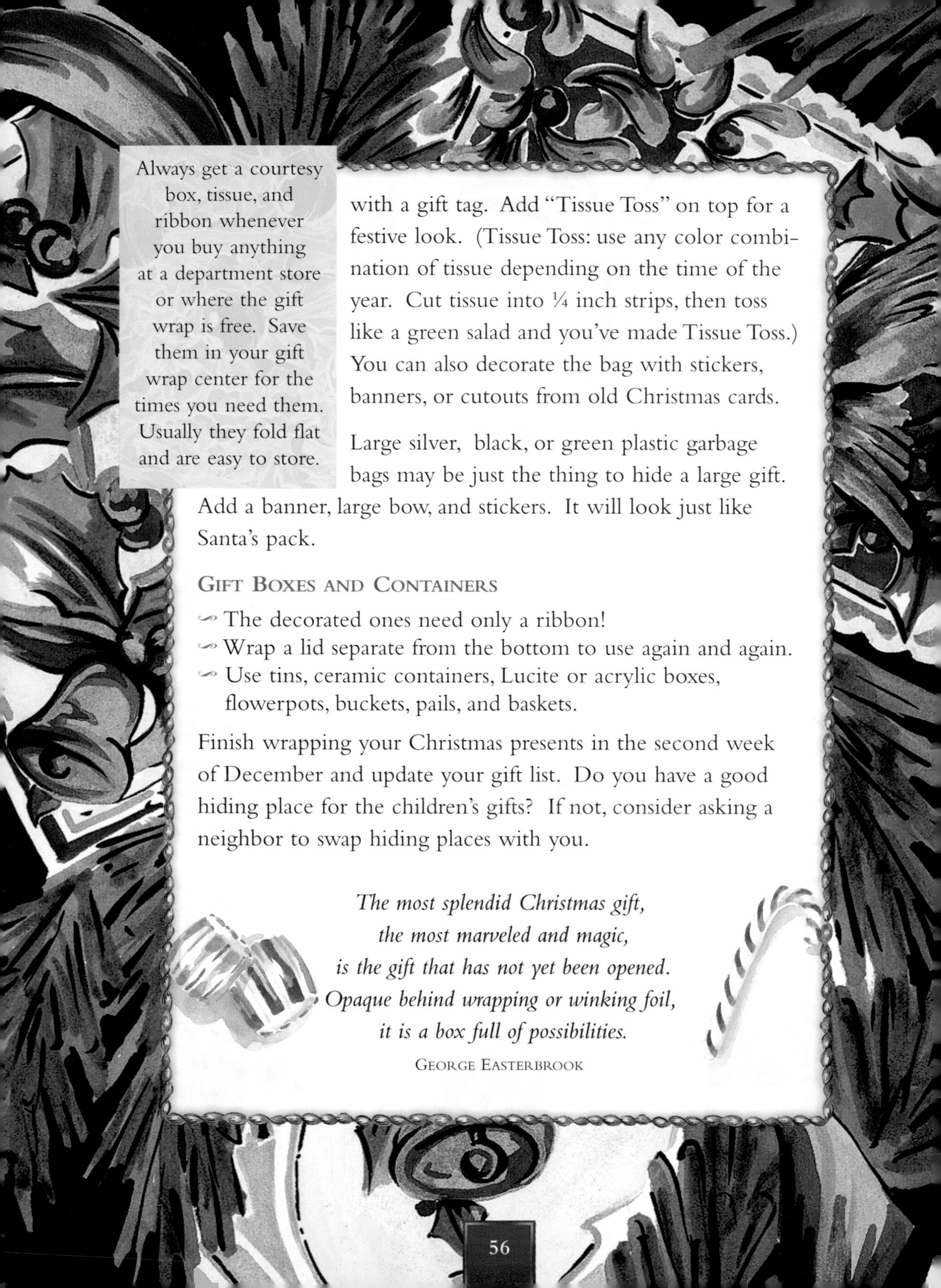

Always get a courtesy box, tissue, and ribbon whenever you buy anything at a department store or where the gift wrap is free. Save them in your gift wrap center for the times you need them. Usually they fold flat and are easy to store.

with a gift tag. Add "Tissue Toss" on top for a festive look. (Tissue Toss: use any color combination of tissue depending on the time of the year. Cut tissue into ¼ inch strips, then toss like a green salad and you've made Tissue Toss.) You can also decorate the bag with stickers, banners, or cutouts from old Christmas cards.

Large silver, black, or green plastic garbage bags may be just the thing to hide a large gift. Add a banner, large bow, and stickers. It will look just like Santa's pack.

Gift Boxes and Containers

- The decorated ones need only a ribbon!
- Wrap a lid separate from the bottom to use again and again.
- Use tins, ceramic containers, Lucite or acrylic boxes, flowerpots, buckets, pails, and baskets.

Finish wrapping your Christmas presents in the second week of December and update your gift list. Do you have a good hiding place for the children's gifts? If not, consider asking a neighbor to swap hiding places with you.

The most splendid Christmas gift,
the most marveled and magic,
is the gift that has not yet been opened.
Opaque behind wrapping or winking foil,
it is a box full of possibilities.

George Easterbrook

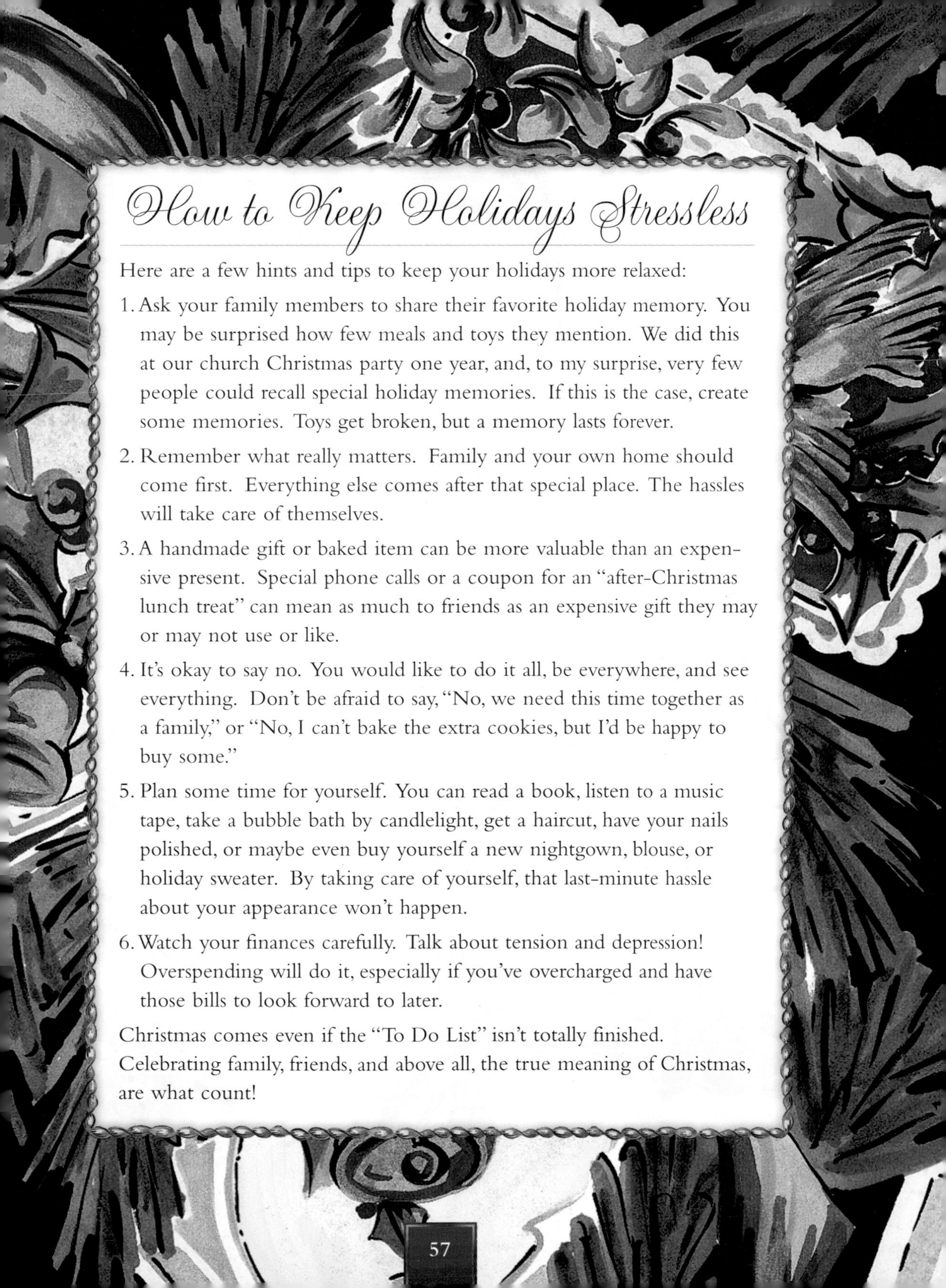

How to Keep Holidays Stressless

Here are a few hints and tips to keep your holidays more relaxed:

1. Ask your family members to share their favorite holiday memory. You may be surprised how few meals and toys they mention. We did this at our church Christmas party one year, and, to my surprise, very few people could recall special holiday memories. If this is the case, create some memories. Toys get broken, but a memory lasts forever.
2. Remember what really matters. Family and your own home should come first. Everything else comes after that special place. The hassles will take care of themselves.
3. A handmade gift or baked item can be more valuable than an expensive present. Special phone calls or a coupon for an "after-Christmas lunch treat" can mean as much to friends as an expensive gift they may or may not use or like.
4. It's okay to say no. You would like to do it all, be everywhere, and see everything. Don't be afraid to say, "No, we need this time together as a family," or "No, I can't bake the extra cookies, but I'd be happy to buy some."
5. Plan some time for yourself. You can read a book, listen to a music tape, take a bubble bath by candlelight, get a haircut, have your nails polished, or maybe even buy yourself a new nightgown, blouse, or holiday sweater. By taking care of yourself, that last-minute hassle about your appearance won't happen.
6. Watch your finances carefully. Talk about tension and depression! Overspending will do it, especially if you've overcharged and have those bills to look forward to later.

Christmas comes even if the "To Do List" isn't totally finished. Celebrating family, friends, and above all, the true meaning of Christmas, are what count!

Now join your hands, and with
your hands your hearts.
SHAKESPEARE

YEAR _____

November

WEEK 4

TO DO LIST

- Package and mail gifts
- Update gift list
- Send out invitations for Christmas parties

Weekly Calendar

Sunday

Monday

Tuesday

Wednesday

Thursday

Friday

Saturday

Shopping List

Tip of the Week

Kitchen gifts are adorable wrapped in a big dish towel and decorated with a copper scouring pad "bow!" And a wooden spoon can be the tag: use a felt pen to write on the handle "to" and "from."

Jo was the first to wake in the gray dawn of Christmas morning. No stockings hung at the fireplace. . . then she remembered her mother's promise, and slipping her hand under her pillow, drew out a little crimson-covered book.

LOUISA MAY ALCOTT
Little Women

YEAR _____

November

WEEK 4

TO DO LIST

- Package and mail gifts
- Update gift list
- Send out invitations for Christmas parties

WEEKLY CALENDAR

SUNDAY

MONDAY

TUESDAY

WEDNESDAY

THURSDAY

FRIDAY

SATURDAY

SHOPPING LIST

Tip of the Week

Rolled giftwrap is the best choice because there are no seams and less waste.

Mrs. Cratchit made the gravy hissing hot, Master Peter mashed the potatoes with incredible vigor, Miss Belinda sweetened up the applesauce, Martha dusted the hot plates, . . . the two younger Cratchits set chairs for everybody, not forgetting themselves. . . .

CHARLES DICKENS, *A Christmas Carol*

YEAR _____

November

WEEK 4

TO DO LIST

- Package and mail gifts
- Update gift list
- Send out invitations for Christmas parties

Weekly Calendar

Sunday

Monday

Tuesday

Wednesday

Thursday

Friday

Saturday

Shopping List

Tip of the Week

Wrapping presents in white paper doesn't have to be dull! Stamp art and stickers are a great way to personalize the wrapping paper, and children love to help.

December
WEEK
1

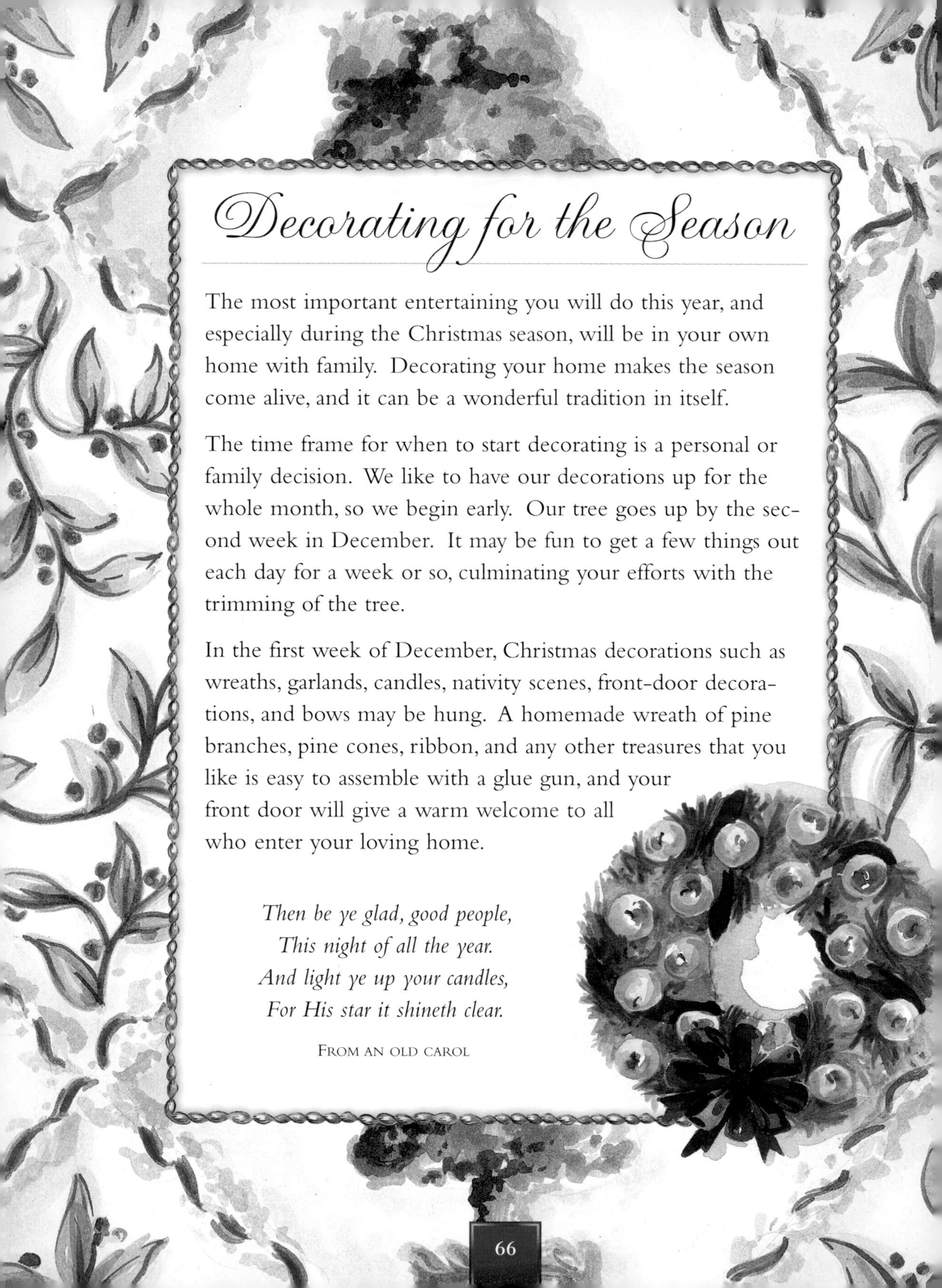

Decorating for the Season

The most important entertaining you will do this year, and especially during the Christmas season, will be in your own home with family. Decorating your home makes the season come alive, and it can be a wonderful tradition in itself.

The time frame for when to start decorating is a personal or family decision. We like to have our decorations up for the whole month, so we begin early. Our tree goes up by the second week in December. It may be fun to get a few things out each day for a week or so, culminating your efforts with the trimming of the tree.

In the first week of December, Christmas decorations such as wreaths, garlands, candles, nativity scenes, front-door decorations, and bows may be hung. A homemade wreath of pine branches, pine cones, ribbon, and any other treasures that you like is easy to assemble with a glue gun, and your front door will give a warm welcome to all who enter your loving home.

Then be ye glad, good people,
This night of all the year.
And light ye up your candles,
For His star it shineth clear.

FROM AN OLD CAROL

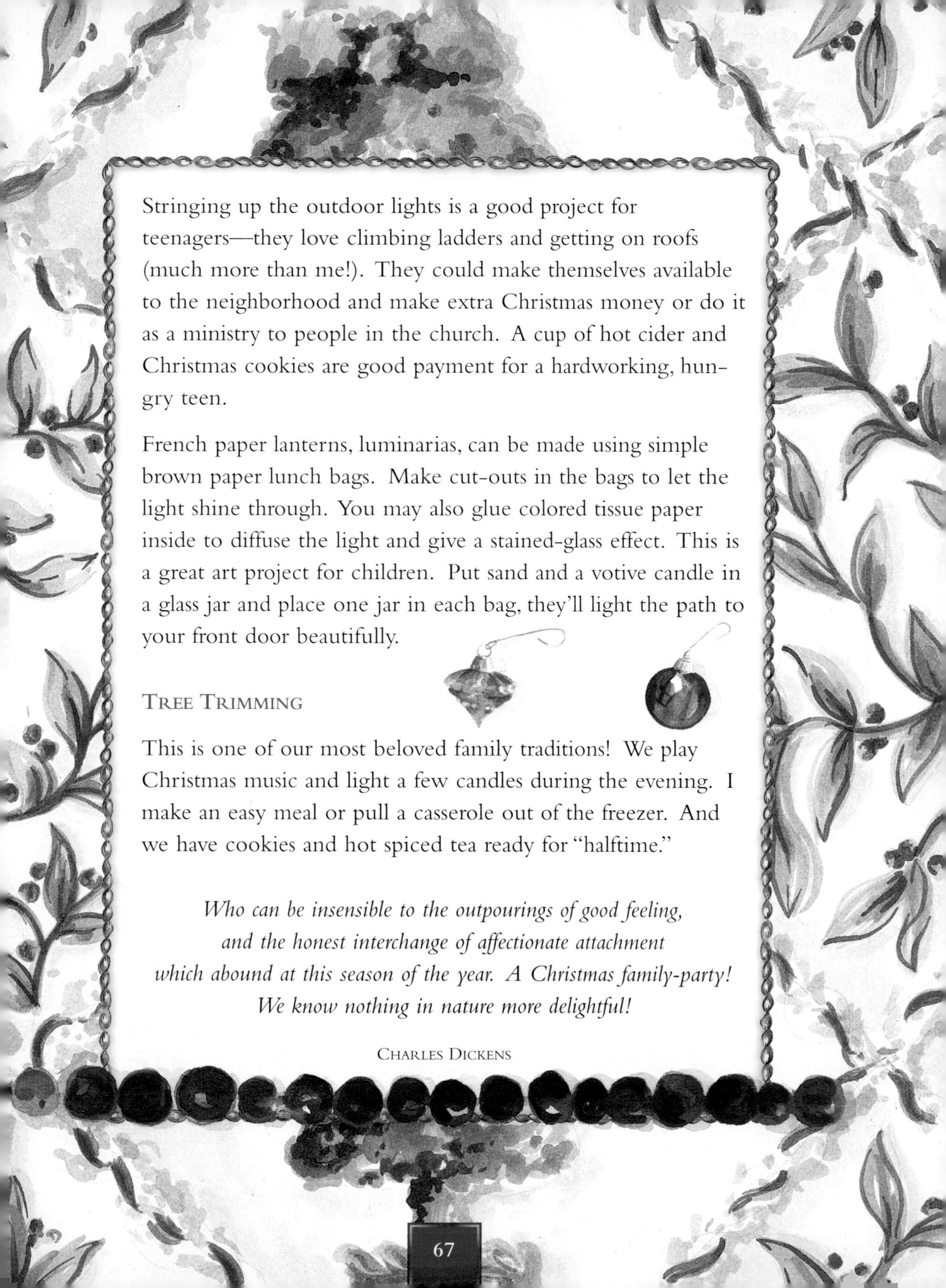

Stringing up the outdoor lights is a good project for teenagers—they love climbing ladders and getting on roofs (much more than me!). They could make themselves available to the neighborhood and make extra Christmas money or do it as a ministry to people in the church. A cup of hot cider and Christmas cookies are good payment for a hardworking, hungry teen.

French paper lanterns, luminarias, can be made using simple brown paper lunch bags. Make cut-outs in the bags to let the light shine through. You may also glue colored tissue paper inside to diffuse the light and give a stained-glass effect. This is a great art project for children. Put sand and a votive candle in a glass jar and place one jar in each bag, they'll light the path to your front door beautifully.

Tree Trimming

This is one of our most beloved family traditions! We play Christmas music and light a few candles during the evening. I make an easy meal or pull a casserole out of the freezer. And we have cookies and hot spiced tea ready for "halftime."

Who can be insensible to the outpourings of good feeling,
and the honest interchange of affectionate attachment
which abound at this season of the year. A Christmas family-party!
We know nothing in nature more delightful!

Charles Dickens

In some parts of the United States, you can go to a tree farm and choose and cut your own tree. We do this every year. It's become a fun tradition. This creates a memory and brings the family together. If no tree farms are available in your area, a tree lot will serve the same purpose. It's also fun to take a picture of your tree untrimmed and then one after it's trimmed.

If you don't want to trim the tree the day you purchase it, keep it in a bucket of water or wet sand. Hose it down to wash off the dust and dirt. It will keep healthy until the time to bring it into the house.

Children can invite friends over so they too can experience this fun evening. After many years, many of our children's friends still recall the special time they had trimming our tree with us. Today our invited friends are our grandchildren. They just love coming over to help us with our tree. They are very curious about our ornaments, and I love sharing the story behind each one.

CANDLES

Candles add a wonderful mood to Christmas decorating. To keep them from tipping over or dripping wax on your furniture, follow these helpful tips:

- Keep candles in the freezer until ready for use. That way they don't have a tendency to drip or spark when lit.
- When candles won't stand up, twist a rubber band around the base before inserting the candle into the holder. Or keep candles firmly in place by putting a little florist's clay in the holder.
- When candles drip on your pretty tablecloths, don't despair! Lay paper towels on the ironing board over and under the drips and iron the wax spots with a medium-to-hot iron. Keep moving the paper towel until the wax is absorbed into them. Presto! The wax is gone and the cloth is saved.

Are you beginning to feel overwhelmed—hustled, hurried, and hassled? If so, prioritize events and extend regrets to those you really don't have to attend. You need time for yourself if you are going to enjoy the next two weeks. It's okay to say no.

This may be the time to pamper yourself a bit. In the first weeks of December, think about your holiday wardrobe. Does anything need to be cleaned, hemmed, pressed, or altered? Do you need to add new accessories to freshen up the old basic Christmas dress? Schedule time for a mid-December hair appointment, manicure, or maybe a massage. Do whatever time and finances will allow, but do treat yourself to a rejuvenating experience, if at all possible. And try to get plenty of sleep and exercise.

Christmas Traditions~ Old and New

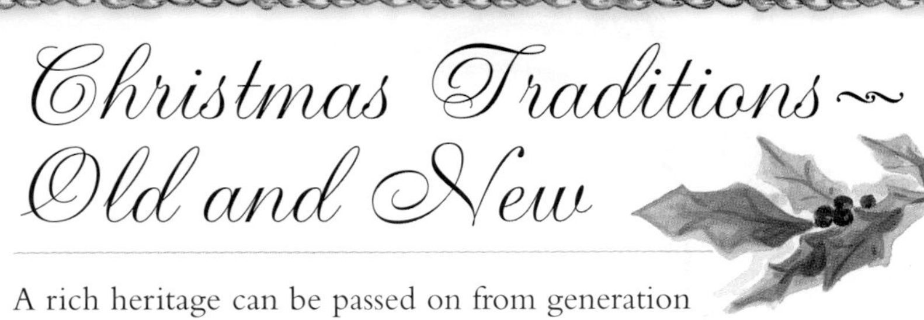

A rich heritage can be passed on from generation to generation with the special traditions that are part of your Christmas celebration, and it's not too late to start now. It makes no difference whether you're a family or an individual—you can still create wonderful memories and establish special traditions.

Let this Christmas be one of happiness, and the New Year
be radiant with hope and filled with the impulse of
doing something for somebody every day.

JOE MITCHELL CHAPPLE

COOKIE EXCHANGE—this is a great idea! Who invented it? We're not really sure, but it was truly a stroke of genius! Instead of making a variety of cookies for the holidays, you can make a large batch of your favorites and swap them for many different kinds.

I received an invitation that instructed me to bring seven dozen cookies plus my recipe written on a recipe card that would be displayed by my cookie plate.

We drank hot Christmas tea and wrote down other recipes on pretty cards from our hostess. Each guest received a paper tote bag (a box or tray could also be used) to take our wonderful collection of goodies home.

MANGER TRADITION—set up a manger scene, homemade from wood or ceramics, or a purchased one. Everything is displayed except the Baby Jesus. Each time a child in the family does a good deed on his own, he gets to put a few pieces of straw in the manger. On Christmas morning,

when there is sufficient straw in the manger, Jesus will appear in His bed. Watch the excitement of the children on Christmas morning when they race to see if the Baby Jesus is there.

Christmas Memory Book—an album dedicated to remembering Christmases is a great idea. All this tradition requires is a photo album. With each year a photo could be added, with the Christmas card sent for the year, and a journal detailing Christmas festivities and traditions. Children may add little mementos if they wish as well.

Family Movies, Videos, Slides—it's so much fun to see those old family movies, slides, photos, or videos. Set aside an evening to do just that. It's interesting to see how everyone has changed.

Advent calendars are great for children. With each day, a little door on the calendar is opened, symbolizing the coming of Christmas day. Our children used to take turns opening a door on our calendar each morning at the breakfast table.

Take a family Christmas photo every year too. We take ours at Thanksgiving. It's the one time we all seem to be together. Coordinating your clothing is also fun. Be creative and do your own thing. Include the pets, teddy bears, and favorite dolls or toys as well. Some of the photos we have of past Christmases delight our grandchildren because *their* parents are hugging dolls and teddy bears!

Enjoy Christmas Cards—ours begin to arrive early in December. We store them in a basket as the days draw closer to Christmas. Then, beginning January 1, we take our card-filled basket to our meal table, and before or after our meal, each member of the family draws out a card. We read the card and who it is from and then offer a prayer for that person or family. This tradition can last well into the new year.

Feed the Homeless—sign up through your church, Salvation Army, or YMCA. In the past, this has been an enjoyable undertaking for our church family. It's a great way to build a better appreciation for what we have while teaching us to help those who are less fortunate.

Give Toys—many local and civic organizations provide an opportunity for individuals and families to donate toys for distribution to needy families on Christmas Eve. Charles Colson's Prison Ministries has a program called "Angel Tree" where you can choose the name of a prisoner's child who has written a Christmas wish. You can then provide this needy child with a gift.

Rent some Christmas classics, get out your fluffiest blankets, and snuggle up with popcorn and cider for a special night. Here are five must-see Christmas videos:

It's a Wonderful Life
A Charlie Brown Christmas
The Bishop's Wife
How the Grinch Stole Christmas
The Fourth Wiseman

Adopt a Family—there are many opportunities where your family can adopt a family in need. Help them with holiday food and gifts—it's a great bridge-builder. This can be done anonymously if it would be easier.

Birthday Party for Jesus—celebrate the birth of Jesus with a party. One mom shared that her family has a birthday cake for Jesus complete with candles. They celebrate Jesus' birthday after the presents are opened on Christmas morning. Another family has a very simple party at the end of Christmas Day. They take ten minutes and sing "Happy Birthday, Jesus," and blow out the candles on the cake. It gives them time to focus on the Baby Jesus.

Put up a "JOY" Stocking—during the month of December, each family member puts thoughts, love notes, and prayers in the "joy" stocking. Then on Christmas Eve or Christmas Day, the notes are pulled out and read. (This would be a great idea to do year-round!)

Christmas traditions don't have to be expensive:

1. Go caroling around the neighborhood or at a convalescent home to spread cheer. Bring a thermos of hot cocoa to keep everyone warm.

2. Visit Santa. Instead of heading to the mall, where lines are apt to be long, visit him at a local small store, library, or firehouse.

3. Bake Christmas cookies for your child's class at school. If you're pressed for time, make the "slice and bake" variety and decorate them with ready-made frosting.

4. Attend a Christmas pageant at your elementary school and take lots of pictures.

5. Enjoy the holiday lights in your hometown on a nighttime walk. It's fun to see your neighbor's decorations. Some towns even have tours.

6. Go to a recital at a local church. Many choirs sing *The Messiah* and other seasonal music.

7. Have a special hot chocolate time, use Christmas mugs. Sprinkle the tops with little marshmallows, whipped cream, and colored sprinkles. Use a candy cane to stir. Yum!

8. Throughout the course of the year, save the remnants of candles from special occasions (birthdays, anniversaries, special dinners, etc.). Melt the remnants to form one large Christmas candle.

9. Look at garage sales, flea markets, and antique shops for pretty, inexpensive teacups to place homemade tea cookies, candies, or tea bags in. Give them as gifts along with a message:

When this cup is empty and the goodies are all gone,
fill it again for another friend, so you can pass it on.

Christmas isn't a season. It's a feeling.

EDNA FERKER

YEAR _____

December

WEEK 1

TO DO LIST

- Decorate for the season
- Finish up Christmas shopping, update "Gifts Given" list
- Plan menu for Christmas parties and Christmas day
- Make up hospitality chart for party
- Finish up the holiday baking

Weekly Calendar

Sunday

Monday

Tuesday

Wednesday

Thursday

Friday

Saturday

Shopping List

Tip of the Week

Remember to purchase needed replacement bulbs and ornament hangers so you are ready for tree trimming.

The great value of traditions comes as they give a family a sense of identity, a belongingness.

DR. JAMES C. DOBSON

YEAR _____

December

WEEK 1

TO DO LIST

- Decorate for the season
- Finish up Christmas shopping, update "Gifts Given" list
- Plan menu for Christmas parties and Christmas day
- Make up hospitality chart for party
- Finish up the holiday baking

Weekly Calendar

Sunday

Monday

Tuesday

Wednesday

Thursday

Friday

Saturday

Shopping List

Tip of the Week

As a family, decide to incorporate one new tradition into your holiday season this year.

Our hearts they hold all Christmas dear,
And earth seems sweet and heaven seems near.

MARJORIE L. C. PICKETHALL

YEAR _____

December

WEEK 1

TO DO LIST

- Decorate for the season
- Finish up Christmas shopping, update "Gifts Given" list
- Plan menu for Christmas parties and Christmas day
- Make up hospitality chart for party
- Finish up the holiday baking

Weekly Calendar

Sunday

Monday

Tuesday

Wednesday

Thursday

Friday

Saturday

Shopping List

Tip of the Week

Invite someone who is alone to celebrate the decorating and festivities, or just a pleasant meal. Elderly people, college students far from home, and singles often miss their families and could use a cheery celebration.

December
WEEK 2

Holiday Fun for Children

Holidays are a fun time for children. They can also be a very hectic time for parents. What with presents, entertaining, cooking, and shopping… the children get so-o-o excited and seem to have more energy than at any other time of the year. Here are some Holiday Helps for children:

- Depending upon the ages of the children, they can help wrap presents. Comic strip sections from newspapers make good wrapping paper, or use white paper or tissue paper that the children can rubber-stamp.
- Gift tags are easily made from last year's Christmas cards. This is a great cut-and-paste project for children. Tags can also be made from matching wrapping paper cut into different shapes: stars, angels, teddy bears, squares, or hearts.
- A great gift children can make is a personalized pillow or pillowcase. Using paint pens in assorted colors or nontoxic acrylic paints, they can decorate the material. Handprints are fun too. The design could also be made on an apron for a grandma.
- Another wonderful gift kids can make is gift certificates. They can be redeemable for doing the dishes, cleaning bedrooms, reading books, or sharing with siblings.

Reading books together is a wonderful treat. Here are five Christmas books you don't want to miss!

- *A Christmas Carol*
  by Charles Dickens
- *One Wintry Night*
  by Ruth Bell Graham
- *24 Days Before Christmas*
  by Madeline L'Engle
- *The Gift of the Magi*
  by O. Henry
- *The Best Christmas Pageant Ever*
  by Barbara Robinson

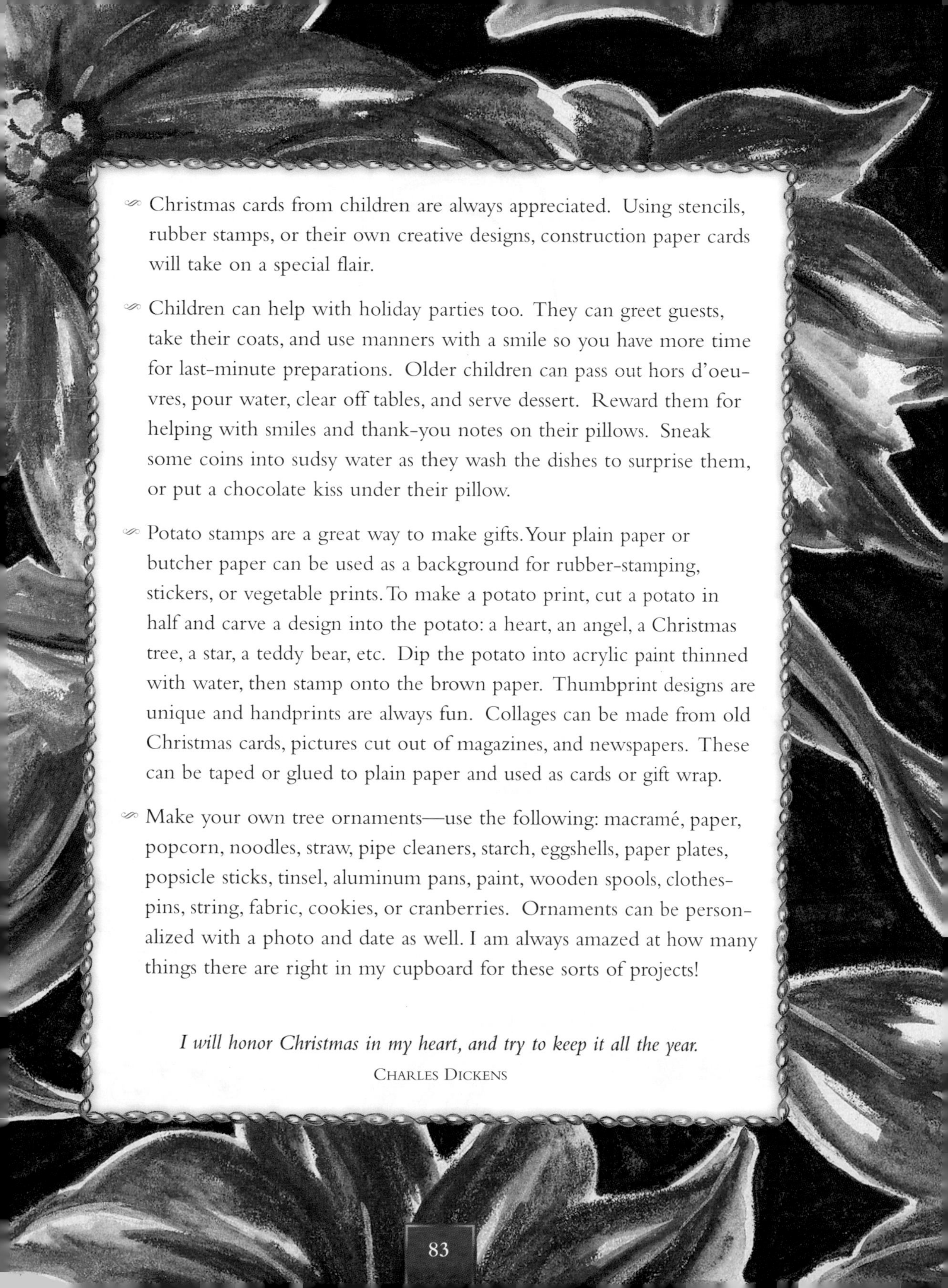

- Christmas cards from children are always appreciated. Using stencils, rubber stamps, or their own creative designs, construction paper cards will take on a special flair.
- Children can help with holiday parties too. They can greet guests, take their coats, and use manners with a smile so you have more time for last-minute preparations. Older children can pass out hors d'oeuvres, pour water, clear off tables, and serve dessert. Reward them for helping with smiles and thank-you notes on their pillows. Sneak some coins into sudsy water as they wash the dishes to surprise them, or put a chocolate kiss under their pillow.
- Potato stamps are a great way to make gifts. Your plain paper or butcher paper can be used as a background for rubber-stamping, stickers, or vegetable prints. To make a potato print, cut a potato in half and carve a design into the potato: a heart, an angel, a Christmas tree, a star, a teddy bear, etc. Dip the potato into acrylic paint thinned with water, then stamp onto the brown paper. Thumbprint designs are unique and handprints are always fun. Collages can be made from old Christmas cards, pictures cut out of magazines, and newspapers. These can be taped or glued to plain paper and used as cards or gift wrap.
- Make your own tree ornaments—use the following: macramé, paper, popcorn, noodles, straw, pipe cleaners, starch, eggshells, paper plates, popsicle sticks, tinsel, aluminum pans, paint, wooden spools, clothespins, string, fabric, cookies, or cranberries. Ornaments can be personalized with a photo and date as well. I am always amazed at how many things there are right in my cupboard for these sorts of projects!

I will honor Christmas in my heart, and try to keep it all the year.

Charles Dickens

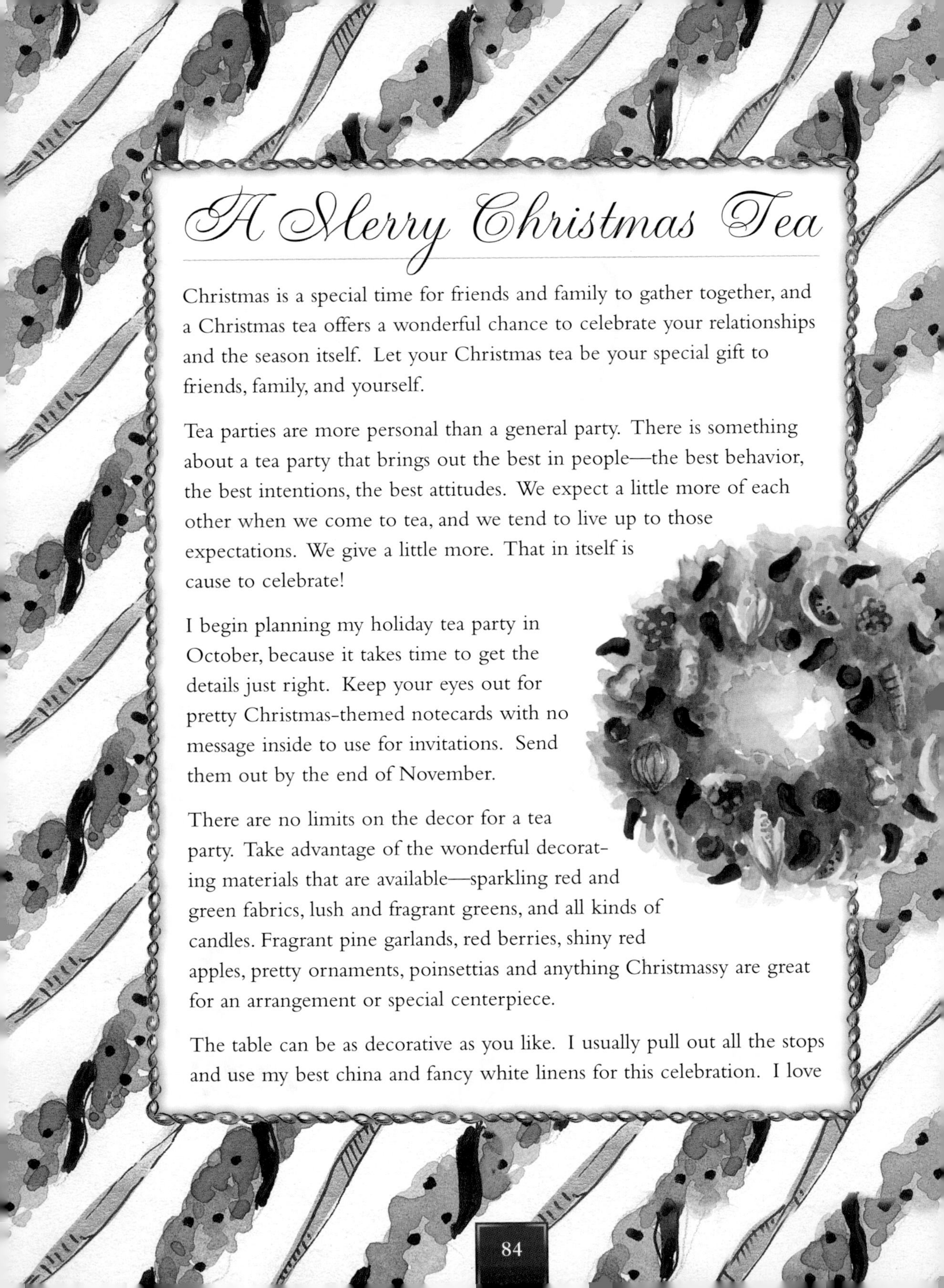

A Merry Christmas Tea

Christmas is a special time for friends and family to gather together, and a Christmas tea offers a wonderful chance to celebrate your relationships and the season itself. Let your Christmas tea be your special gift to friends, family, and yourself.

Tea parties are more personal than a general party. There is something about a tea party that brings out the best in people—the best behavior, the best intentions, the best attitudes. We expect a little more of each other when we come to tea, and we tend to live up to those expectations. We give a little more. That in itself is cause to celebrate!

I begin planning my holiday tea party in October, because it takes time to get the details just right. Keep your eyes out for pretty Christmas-themed notecards with no message inside to use for invitations. Send them out by the end of November.

There are no limits on the decor for a tea party. Take advantage of the wonderful decorating materials that are available—sparkling red and green fabrics, lush and fragrant greens, and all kinds of candles. Fragrant pine garlands, red berries, shiny red apples, pretty ornaments, poinsettias and anything Christmassy are great for an arrangement or special centerpiece.

The table can be as decorative as you like. I usually pull out all the stops and use my best china and fancy white linens for this celebration. I love

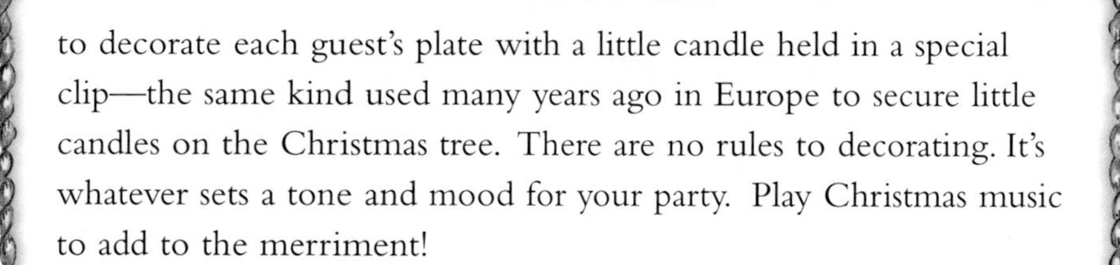

to decorate each guest's plate with a little candle held in a special clip—the same kind used many years ago in Europe to secure little candles on the Christmas tree. There are no rules to decorating. It's whatever sets a tone and mood for your party. Play Christmas music to add to the merriment!

And load the table with a variety of sweet and savory foods. I usually have a special tea, some tea sandwiches, a fancy cake, fruits and a special cheese, like mascarpone, and decorated Christmas cookies. Everything is presented on doily-lined trays…it's almost too pretty to eat!

Spiced Russian Tea

- 6 teaspoons Russian blend or any good black tea
- 1 pinch cloves
- 1½ pints freshly boiled water

Place tea and cloves in pot, add water, and brew for five minutes before pouring. Add sugar and lemon to taste.

The most special part of this holiday tea is when we share our favorite memories and Christmas blessings together. I light the candle of the person nearest to me and ask her to share a Christmas thought or Christmas blessing. After she speaks, she lights the candle of the person next to her, who then shares her Christmas thoughts. Around the room we go, with each person sharing a bit of her heart.

Almond Chicken Tea Sandwiches

- 3 boneless, skinless chicken breasts, cooked and chopped coarsely
- ½ cup slivered, blanched almonds
- ½ cup mayonnaise
- White or wheat bread

Mix chicken, almonds, and mayonnaise.

Butter each slice of bread well. On half the slices, spoon about 3 tablespoons of almond chicken mixture. Top with remaining slices.

Wrap in wax paper and again in a slightly dampened kitchen towel. Let filling set for at least an hour before serving. Cut off crusts and trim into pretty shapes.

Sweet courtesy has done its most if you have made each guest forget that he himself is not the host.

THOMAS BAILEY ALDRICH

YEAR _____

December

WEEK 2

TO DO LIST

- Buy and trim the Christmas tree
- Review calendar, prioritize invitations, programs and other commitments
- Check catalog orders (prepare plan B if necessary)
- Cook and freeze appetizers for the party
- Finish all wrapping and hide presents or place under the tree

Weekly Calendar

Sunday

Monday

Tuesday

Wednesday

Thursday

Friday

Saturday

Shopping List

Tip of the Week

Leftover fabrics and laces are great materials for Christmas presents. Children could make a tie for dad or a collar for mom.

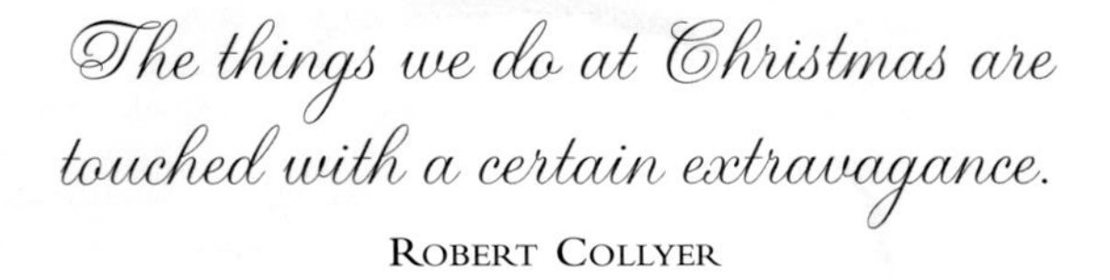

YEAR _____

December

WEEK 2

TO DO LIST

- Buy and trim the Christmas tree
- Review calendar, prioritize invitations, programs and other commitments
- Check catalog orders (prepare plan B if necessary)
- Cook and freeze appetizers for the party
- Finish all wrapping and hide presents or place under the tree

Weekly Calendar

Sunday

Monday

Tuesday

Wednesday

Thursday

Friday

Saturday

Shopping List

Tip of the Week

It's fun to prepare your own tea goodies, but there's nothing wrong with buying them. Try a bakery, deli, or tea shop for delicious edibles.

At Christmas be merry, and thankful withal, And feast thy poor neighbors, the great with the small.

THOMAS TUSSER

YEAR _____

December

WEEK 2

TO DO LIST

- Buy and trim the Christmas tree
- Review calendar, prioritize invitations, programs and other commitments
- Check catalog orders (prepare plan B if necessary)
- Cook and freeze appetizers for the party
- Finish all wrapping and hide presents or place under the tree

Weekly Calendar

Sunday

Monday

Tuesday

Wednesday

Thursday

Friday

Saturday

Shopping List

Tip of the Week

If you have snow, make a snowman in the yard with your children. For a very merry snowman, fill several spray bottles with water and food coloring (especially red and green!).

December

WEEK 3

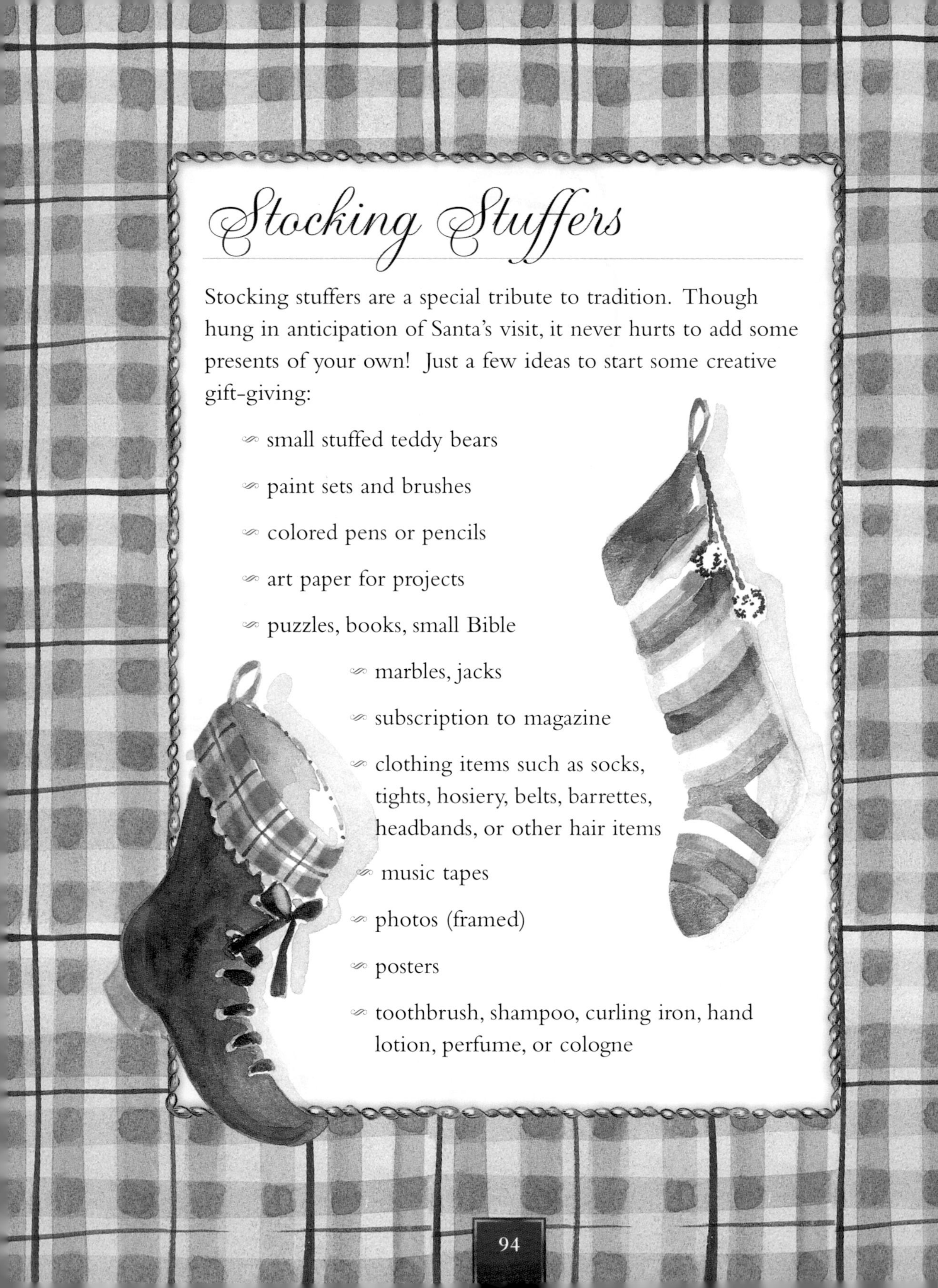

Stocking Stuffers

Stocking stuffers are a special tribute to tradition. Though hung in anticipation of Santa's visit, it never hurts to add some presents of your own! Just a few ideas to start some creative gift-giving:

- small stuffed teddy bears
- paint sets and brushes
- colored pens or pencils
- art paper for projects
- puzzles, books, small Bible
- marbles, jacks
- subscription to magazine
- clothing items such as socks, tights, hosiery, belts, barrettes, headbands, or other hair items
- music tapes
- photos (framed)
- posters
- toothbrush, shampoo, curling iron, hand lotion, perfume, or cologne

- kitchen items for mom
- small garden tools and packaged seeds for dad
- nuts and fruits
- balloons with a dollar bill tucked inside
- theater tickets for a special play
- golf balls
- tennis balls
- measuring tape
- flashlight
- etc. etc. etc.…This should get you started with suggested ideas!

The Story of the Stocking

Legend says the custom of hanging stockings was inspired by Saint Nick himself. The three daughters of a poor man could not marry well without a suitable dowry. On a cold December eve, the eldest daughter found a purse shaped like a stocking, filled with gold. The next night, another stocking of gold was found by the second daughter. And on the third night, Christmas Eve, the father caught Saint Nicholas in the act of throwing a third stocking of gold into the window for the youngest girl.

Ever after, children have hung stockings for Saint Nicholas to fill them with presents and surprises for Christmas morning.

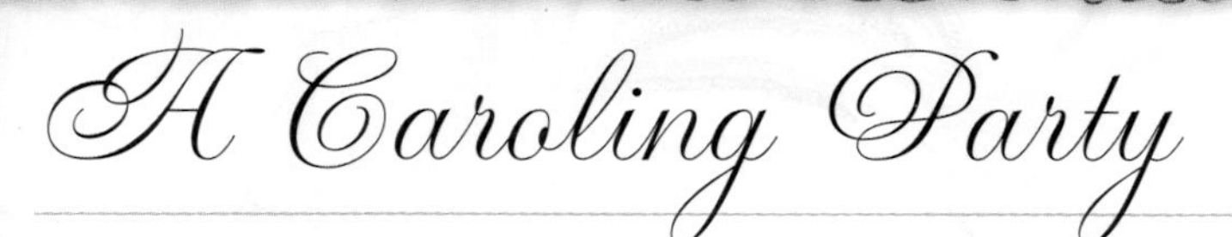

A Caroling Party

I love the feeling of spreading the special sounds of Christmas to friends and neighbors. Every year we do this, either through a church function or on our own with friends. It's a great way to spread joy to those who may not be able to celebrate with family and friends. One of our yearly stops is at a rest home, and every year they anticipate the event almost as much as I do.

Traditional holiday caroling started in 1660 in England. Many of the carols we know, like *Joy To The World, O Come All Ye Faithful*, and *Silent Night* were not written until the 1800s.

Gather together a small group of friends to go caroling. Singing old songs with friends puts the holiday into perspective. Off-tune voices disappear as peace and good-will tidings fill the air.

Many people know the verses of traditional carols by heart, but you may want to type out the words to several songs and paste them into bright red and green folders. It's a good idea to have a practice run-through to decide what songs to sing. Other fun ideas for "old-fashioned" caroling:

- Have everyone wear bright scarves or hats
- Wear bells on your shoelaces or carry bells
- Carry candles or flashlights

Choose a neighborhood of someone in the group to spread your good cheer, and include a rest home or shut-in too. And when it's cold, bring a thermos of hot chocolate along to keep everyone warm. We usually end the night with cookies and cider around a warming fire at someone's home to talk about the carols and what they mean.

THE BIRTH OF *SILENT NIGHT*

On December 23, 1818, in the village of Oberndorf, Austria, church organist Franz Gruber and priest Father Mohr discovered a mouse-gnawed hole in the leather bellows of the church organ. Both knew that a Christmas Eve service without music was unthinkable!

Franz shyly gave the priest a small poem he had written and asked Father Mohr to set the poem to music. The children's choir would then perform the little piece for this special service.

Father Mohr strummed his guitar and came up with a lilting tune to fit the very special words of this new song. That afternoon, he and Franz gathered with the 12 little boys and girls to rehearse.

On Christmas Eve the children sang the verses to *Silent Night* with clear voices, and a beloved carol was born.

HOT COCOA MIX RECIPE

1 8-quart box powdered milk
1 6-ounce jar Cremora®
1 1-pound box Nestlés® Quik
2 teaspoons cinnamon

Mix all ingredients together in a large bowl. Add 3 heaping tablespoons of hot cocoa mix to a mug full of hot water and stir.

At Christmas play and make good cheer,
For Christmas comes but once a year.

THOMAS TUSSER

YEAR _____

December

WEEK 3

TO DO LIST

- Double check stocking stuffers. Do you have enough?
- Review hospitality list
- Spend some time relaxing with a special activity just for you
- Make holiday calls to avoid busy phone lines next week

Weekly Calendar

Sunday

Monday

Tuesday

Wednesday

Thursday

Friday

Saturday

Shopping List

Tip of the Week

Make simple ornaments to give the people you visit. Or, if you are visiting shut-ins, bring a small basket of cookies or gift certificates for your time!

Here we come a~wassailing among the leaves so green,
Here we come a wand'ring, so fair to be seen...
AN ENGLISH CAROL

YEAR _____

December

WEEK 3

TO DO LIST

- Double check stocking stuffers. Do you have enough?
- Review hospitality list
- Spend some time relaxing with a special activity just for you
- Make holiday calls to avoid busy phone lines next week

Weekly Calendar

Sunday

Monday

Tuesday

Wednesday

Thursday

Friday

Saturday

Shopping List

Tip of the Week

Have a Caroling Kidnapping Party! Start with a small group of carolers. Stop at friends' houses first, sing to them, and then "kidnap" them to join the group. Once the group is complete, continue caroling until you return to your house where warm cider and delicious snacks await.

You will be with child and give birth to a son,
and you are to give him the name Jesus.

THE BOOK OF LUKE

YEAR _____

December

WEEK 3

TO DO LIST

- Double check stocking stuffers. Do you have enough?
- Review hospitality list
- Spend some time relaxing with a special activity just for you
- Make holiday calls to avoid busy phone lines next week

Weekly Calendar

Sunday

Monday

Tuesday

Wednesday

Thursday

Friday

Saturday

Shopping List

Tip of the Week

Use stockings to enrich Christmas-giving by hanging one especially for gifts of love. Have each person add a written promise to give—support for a hungry child, volunteer hours at a local soup kitchen, or visits to a lonely neighbor.

December

WEEK 4

Special Things to Do on Christmas Eve and Christmas Day

Every family has certain traditions for how to spend Christmas. Here are a few ideas to inspire new traditions for a wonderful Christmas Eve and Christmas day:

- Before bedtime, hide new pajamas for each family member in their bedrooms. Let everyone find their PJs, then gather together for the hanging of the stockings. (Having new pajamas makes for nice pictures on Christmas morning too!)
- Gather everyone around the fireplace and read *'Twas the Night Before Christmas* or the Christmas Story from the Bible.
- Attend a Christmas Eve church service.
- Instead of going to bed on time, bundle up in warm clothes and sit in the backyard. Look at the stars and talk about the Star of Bethlehem.
- Celebrate an old Victorian tradition that began in Germany. The last ornament to be hung on the tree on Christmas Eve is a glass pickle ornament. Hide it carefully. The first person to find that special ornament on Christmas morning receives a special surprise from St. Nick.
- On Christmas Eve, wrap a small gift for each person in layers

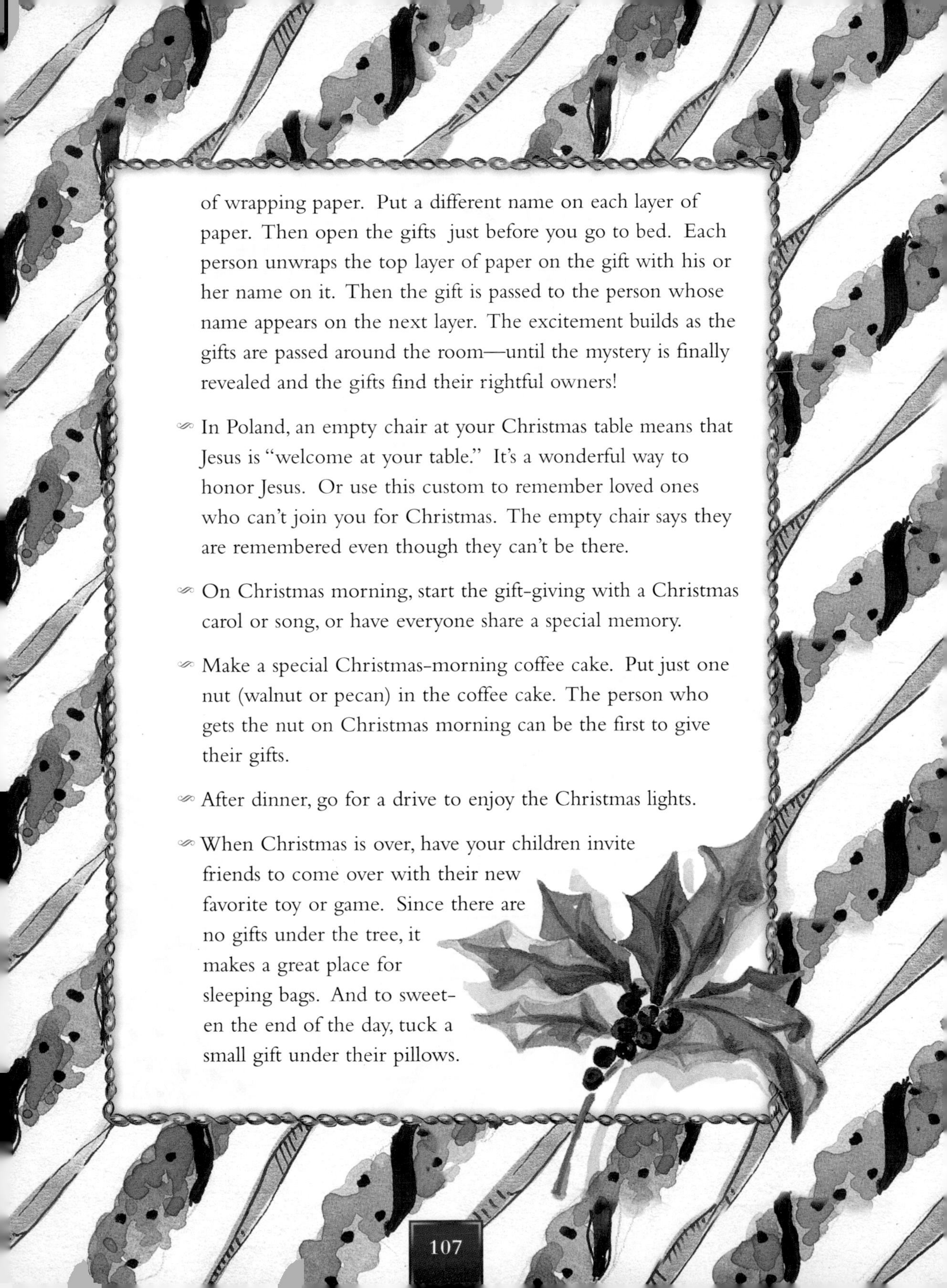

of wrapping paper. Put a different name on each layer of paper. Then open the gifts just before you go to bed. Each person unwraps the top layer of paper on the gift with his or her name on it. Then the gift is passed to the person whose name appears on the next layer. The excitement builds as the gifts are passed around the room—until the mystery is finally revealed and the gifts find their rightful owners!

- In Poland, an empty chair at your Christmas table means that Jesus is "welcome at your table." It's a wonderful way to honor Jesus. Or use this custom to remember loved ones who can't join you for Christmas. The empty chair says they are remembered even though they can't be there.
- On Christmas morning, start the gift-giving with a Christmas carol or song, or have everyone share a special memory.
- Make a special Christmas-morning coffee cake. Put just one nut (walnut or pecan) in the coffee cake. The person who gets the nut on Christmas morning can be the first to give their gifts.
- After dinner, go for a drive to enjoy the Christmas lights.
- When Christmas is over, have your children invite friends to come over with their new favorite toy or game. Since there are no gifts under the tree, it makes a great place for sleeping bags. And to sweeten the end of the day, tuck a small gift under their pillows.

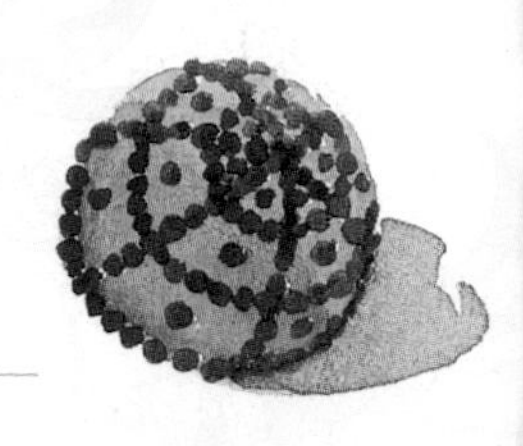

When you need decorating ideas and are pressed for time, here are some great tips to dress up your home for Christmas:

- Spicy oranges make everything smell good, and they're so easy to make. Poke holes all over an orange with a toothpick, create a pretty design. Then push a whole clove into each hole. Roll the orange in orris root (found at craft stores) and place in a decorative bowl with some pine branches.
- Hospitality baskets tell everyone they are welcome. Keep a supply of wrapped goodies in a decorated basket by the front door. Whenever friends stop by, share a gift with them. Presents could be homemade treats like hot cocoa mix, cookies and candies packaged in jars, wrapped ornaments, wooden spoons, or fancy teas.
- Tie a few bells to the end of some ribbon and tie the ribbon around your door knob. Every time someone comes in, a cheery jingle will remind you it's Christmas!
- Spread evergreens, holly berries, ivy, twigs, and pine cones in your window boxes for some beautiful natural decorations.

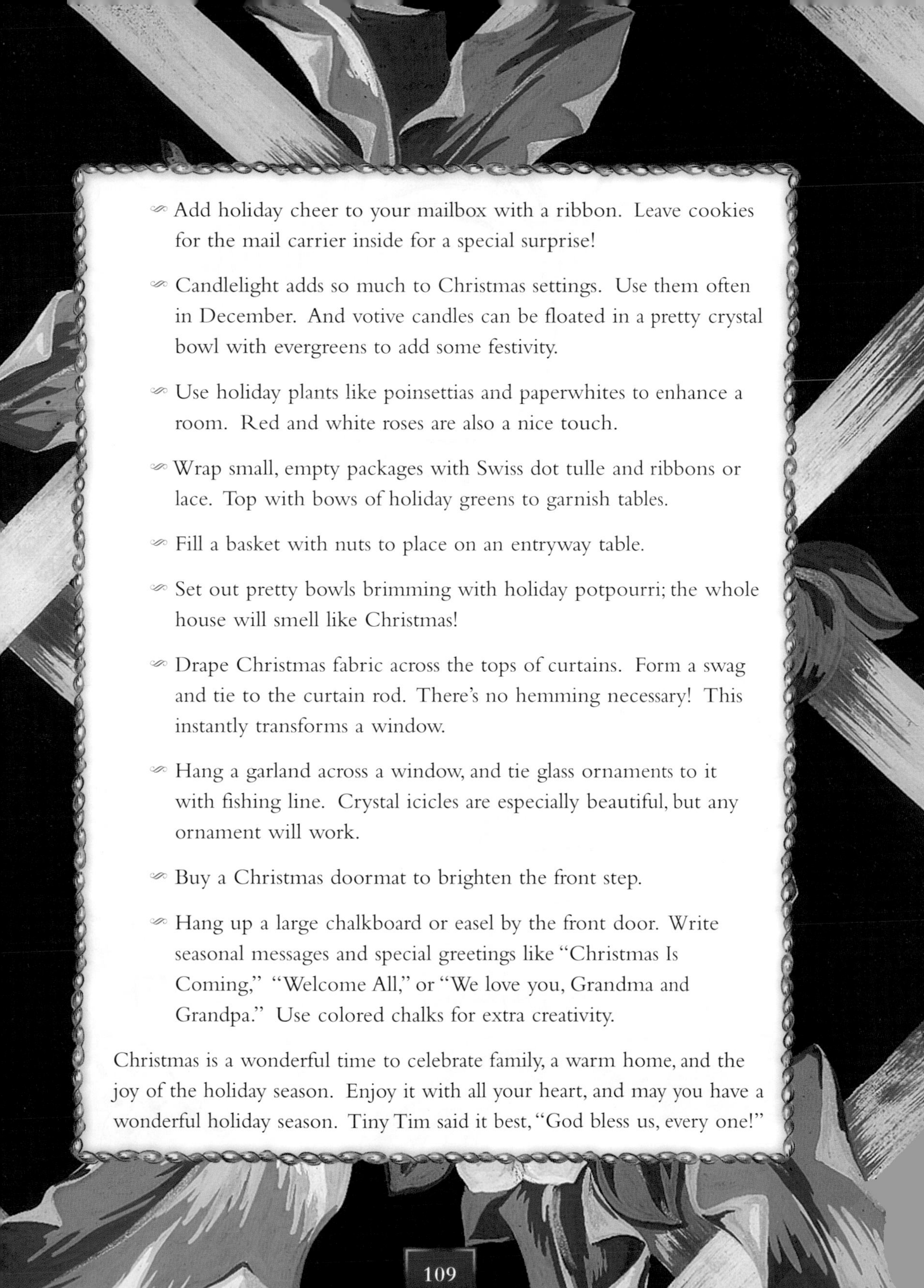

- Add holiday cheer to your mailbox with a ribbon. Leave cookies for the mail carrier inside for a special surprise!
- Candlelight adds so much to Christmas settings. Use them often in December. And votive candles can be floated in a pretty crystal bowl with evergreens to add some festivity.
- Use holiday plants like poinsettias and paperwhites to enhance a room. Red and white roses are also a nice touch.
- Wrap small, empty packages with Swiss dot tulle and ribbons or lace. Top with bows of holiday greens to garnish tables.
- Fill a basket with nuts to place on an entryway table.
- Set out pretty bowls brimming with holiday potpourri; the whole house will smell like Christmas!
- Drape Christmas fabric across the tops of curtains. Form a swag and tie to the curtain rod. There's no hemming necessary! This instantly transforms a window.
- Hang a garland across a window, and tie glass ornaments to it with fishing line. Crystal icicles are especially beautiful, but any ornament will work.
- Buy a Christmas doormat to brighten the front step.
- Hang up a large chalkboard or easel by the front door. Write seasonal messages and special greetings like "Christmas Is Coming," "Welcome All," or "We love you, Grandma and Grandpa." Use colored chalks for extra creativity.

Christmas is a wonderful time to celebrate family, a warm home, and the joy of the holiday season. Enjoy it with all your heart, and may you have a wonderful holiday season. Tiny Tim said it best, "God bless us, every one!"

And she brought forth her firstborn Son, and wrapped Him in swaddling cloths, and laid Him in a manger, because there was no room for them in the inn.

THE BOOK OF LUKE

YEAR _____

December

WEEK 4

TO DO LIST

- Celebrate a new tradition
- Deliver plates of your baked gifts to friends or neighbors
- Enjoy your family! Merry Christmas!

Weekly Calendar

Sunday

Monday

Tuesday

Wednesday

Thursday

Friday

Saturday

Shopping List

Tip of the Week

Feed the birds with your Christmas tree! After the holiday, remove all the decorations, especially tinsel. Pinecones can be filled with peanut butter and added to the tree. Drizzle honey over tree to share a sweet treat. Leave the popcorn and cranberry garlands. The birds love them!

Running to the window, he opened it, and put out his head...
Golden sunlight; Heavenly sky; sweet fresh air; merry bells.
Oh glorious! Glorious!... Christmas Day!

CHARLES DICKENS

YEAR _____

December

WEEK 4

TO DO LIST

- Celebrate a new tradition
- Deliver plates of your baked gifts to friends or neighbors
- Enjoy your family! Merry Christmas!

Weekly Calendar

Sunday

Monday

Tuesday

Wednesday

Thursday

Friday

Saturday

Shopping List

Tip of the Week

Have a Christmas Eve buffet with a special dish prepared by each member of the family. In the week before Christmas, each member can plan their specific dish while keeping it a secret from everyone until the dinner.

May Christmas blessings on thee shine,
And joy and peace be always thine.

ANONYMOUS

YEAR _____

December

WEEK 4

TO DO LIST

- Celebrate a new tradition
- Deliver plates of your baked gifts to friends or neighbors
- Enjoy your family! Merry Christmas!

Weekly Calendar

Sunday

Monday

Tuesday

Wednesday

Thursday

Friday

Saturday

Shopping List

Tip of the Week

Even the bathroom can be festive! Decorate a pretty basket and fill with Christmassy red and green soaps.

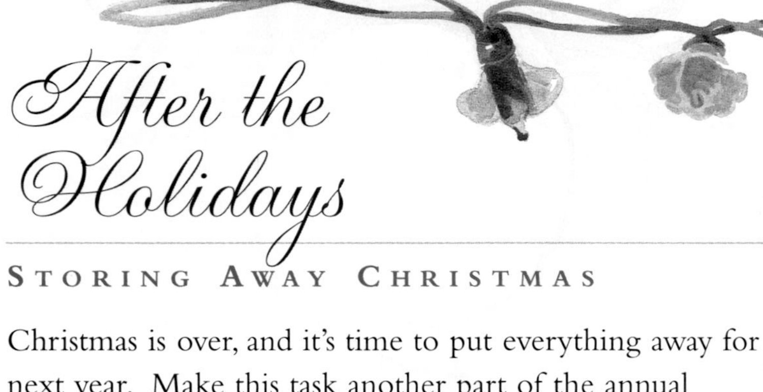

After the Holidays

Storing Away Christmas

Christmas is over, and it's time to put everything away for next year. Make this task another part of the annual festivities, a job the whole family can enjoy together. Play music as you put Christmas away, and be sure to have rewards on hand for deserving helpers. Take a break for cookies or some other treat—make it fun!

Christmas is *big* in our home, and it takes 12 medium boxes, four marked trash bags, and four oversized boxes to put it all away! I use an easy system to keep track of where I store everything. With some simple planning, you can organize your Christmas trimmings.

Here's what you'll need:

- A good supply of sturdy boxes
- 1 wide black felt-tip pen
- 3 x 5 cards
- 3 x 5 card file box

Instead of writing a description of the contents on the storage box, simply number your boxes. Then on a 3 x 5 card, write the box number, the specific contents, and where the box is located. If box #3 had my Christmas village in it, my index card labeled #3 would look like this:

#3

GARAGE, TOP SHELF

Christmas Village

Keep the cards in a file box. That's all there is to it!

Store garlands, wreaths, and candles separately, so you can reach them without sorting through tree-trimming items. Wreaths store wonderfully in plastic trash bags. They can be labeled as if they were boxes by stapling a 3 x 5 card to the bag. Crunched up newspapers make a great cushion for fragile decorations, and they can be used year after year.

When the season comes, pull out your file box. You'll be ready to find exactly what you need when you need it. Decorating next year will be a snap!

Christmas Card Record

Name	Address	Year	Sent	Rec'd

Christmas Card Record

Name	Address	Year	Sent	Rec'd

Christmas Card Record

Name	Address	Year	Sent	Rec'd

Christmas Card Record

Name	Address	Year	Sent	Rec'd

Christmas Card Record

Name	Address	Year	Sent	Rec'd

Christmas Card Record

Name	Address	Year	Sent	Rec'd

Christmas Card Record

Name	Address	Year	Sent	Rec'd

Christmas Card Record

NAME	ADDRESS	YEAR	SENT	REC'D

Gifts Given

To	Gift	Year

Gifts Given

To	Gift	Year

Gifts Given

To	Gift	Year

Gifts Received

GIFT	TO	FROM	THANK YOU

Gifts Received

Gift	To	From	Thank You

Gifts Received

Gift	To	From	Thank You

Shopping Guide

	Sizes			
Name	Dress/Suit	Shirt/Sweater	Pants	Favorites

Shopping Guide

	SIZES			
NAME	DRESS/SUIT	SHIRT/SWEATER	PANTS	FAVORITES

On Order List

Date Ordered	For	Item	Company	Received

On Order List

Date Ordered	For	Item	Company	Received

Christmas Party Hospitality Chart

DATE: ______________________ PLACE: ______________________

TIME: ______________________ NUMBER OF GUESTS: ______________________

Things to do	✓	Menu:
Last week of November:		Appetizers:
Send out invitations		
First week of December:		
Plan centerpiece		
Prepare menu		Entree:
Make shopping list		
Second week of December:		Side dishes:
Shop for ingredients/decorations		
Bake/prepare food and freeze		
Check RSVP list		
		Salad:
Three days before:		
Polish silver		
Clean house as needed		Dessert:
Prepare garnishes, chop nuts		
Review menu, check ingredients		
		Drinks:
One day before:		
Prep veggies, make trays		Guest list: RSVP:
Defrost appetizers and goodies		
Set table		
Cook main course, hot dishes		
Clean up house		
Day of party:		
Make punch		
Make up trays, add garnish		
Warm up hot dishes		
Last minute:		
Put out relishes		
Light candles		
Play music		

Christmas Party Hospitality Chart

Date: ______________________ Place: ______________________

Time: ______________________ Number of guests: ______________________

Things to do	✓	Menu:
Last week of November:		Appetizers:
Send out invitations		
First week of December:		
Plan centerpiece		
Prepare menu		Entree:
Make shopping list		
Second week of December:		Side dishes:
Shop for ingredients/decorations		
Bake/prepare food and freeze		
Check RSVP list		
		Salad:
Three days before:		
Polish silver		
Clean house as needed		Dessert:
Prepare garnishes, chop nuts		
Review menu, check ingredients		
		Drinks:
One day before:		
Prep veggies, make trays		Guest list: RSVP:
Defrost appetizers and goodies		
Set table		
Cook main course, hot dishes		
Clean up house		
Day of party:		
Make punch		
Make up trays, add garnish		
Warm up hot dishes		
Last minute:		
Put out relishes		
Light candles		
Play music		

Christmas Party Hospitality Chart

DATE: ______________________ PLACE: ______________________

TIME: ______________________ NUMBER OF GUESTS: ______________________

Things to do	✓	Menu:
Last week of November:		Appetizers:
Send out invitations		
First week of December:		
Plan centerpiece		
Prepare menu		Entree:
Make shopping list		
Second week of December:		Side dishes:
Shop for ingredients/decorations		
Bake/prepare food and freeze		
Check RSVP list		
		Salad:
Three days before:		
Polish silver		
Clean house as needed		Dessert:
Prepare garnishes, chop nuts		
Review menu, check ingredients		
		Drinks:
One day before:		
Prep veggies, make trays		Guest list: RSVP:
Defrost appetizers and goodies		
Set table		
Cook main course, hot dishes		
Clean up house		
Day of party:		
Make punch		
Make up trays, add garnish		
Warm up hot dishes		
Last minute:		
Put out relishes		
Light candles		
Play music		

Christmas Party Hospitality Chart

DATE: ______________________ PLACE: ______________________

TIME: ______________________ NUMBER OF GUESTS: ______________________

Things to do	✓	Menu:
Last week of November:		Appetizers:
Send out invitations		
First week of December:		
Plan centerpiece		
Prepare menu		Entree:
Make shopping list		
Second week of December:		Side dishes:
Shop for ingredients/decorations		
Bake/prepare food and freeze		
Check RSVP list		
		Salad:
Three days before:		
Polish silver		
Clean house as needed		Dessert:
Prepare garnishes, chop nuts		
Review menu, check ingredients		
		Drinks:
One day before:		
Prep veggies, make trays		Guest list: RSVP:
Defrost appetizers and goodies		
Set table		
Cook main course, hot dishes		
Clean up house		
Day of party:		
Make punch		
Make up trays, add garnish		
Warm up hot dishes		
Last minute:		
Put out relishes		
Light candles		
Play music		

Christmas Party Hospitality Chart

DATE: ____________________ PLACE: ____________________

TIME: ____________________ NUMBER OF GUESTS: ____________________

Things to do	✓	Menu:
Last week of November:		Appetizers:
Send out invitations		
First week of December:		
Plan centerpiece		
Prepare menu		Entree:
Make shopping list		
Second week of December:		Side dishes:
Shop for ingredients/decorations		
Bake/prepare food and freeze		
Check RSVP list		
		Salad:
Three days before:		
Polish silver		
Clean house as needed		Dessert:
Prepare garnishes, chop nuts		
Review menu, check ingredients		
		Drinks:
One day before:		
Prep veggies, make trays		Guest list: RSVP:
Defrost appetizers and goodies		
Set table		
Cook main course, hot dishes		
Clean up house		
Day of party:		
Make punch		
Make up trays, add garnish		
Warm up hot dishes		
Last minute:		
Put out relishes		
Light candles		
Play music		

Christmas Party Hospitality Chart

Date:	Place:
Time:	Number of guests:

Things to do	✓	Menu:
Last week of November:		Appetizers:
Send out invitations		
First week of December:		
Plan centerpiece		
Prepare menu		Entree:
Make shopping list		
Second week of December:		Side dishes:
Shop for ingredients/decorations		
Bake/prepare food and freeze		
Check RSVP list		
		Salad:
Three days before:		
Polish silver		
Clean house as needed		Dessert:
Prepare garnishes, chop nuts		
Review menu, check ingredients		
		Drinks:
One day before:		
Prep veggies, make trays		Guest list: RSVP:
Defrost appetizers and goodies		
Set table		
Cook main course, hot dishes		
Clean up house		
Day of party:		
Make punch		
Make up trays, add garnish		
Warm up hot dishes		
Last minute:		
Put out relishes		
Light candles		
Play music		

Important Phone Numbers

Name	Phone Number

Important Phone Numbers

Name	Phone Number

1998

JANUARY

S	M	T	W	T	F	S
				1	2	3
4	5	6	7	8	9	10
11	12	13	14	15	16	17
18	19	20	21	22	23	24
25	26	27	28	29	30	31

FEBRUARY

S	M	T	W	T	F	S
1	2	3	4	5	6	7
8	9	10	11	12	13	14
15	16	17	18	19	20	21
22	23	24	25	26	27	28

MARCH

S	M	T	W	T	F	S
1	2	3	4	5	6	7
8	9	10	11	12	13	14
15	16	17	18	19	20	21
22	23	24	25	26	27	28
29	30	31				

APRIL

S	M	T	W	T	F	S
			1	2	3	4
5	6	7	8	9	10	11
12	13	14	15	16	17	18
19	20	21	22	23	24	25
26	27	28	29	30		

MAY

S	M	T	W	T	F	S
					1	2
3	4	5	6	7	8	9
10	11	12	13	14	15	16
17	18	19	20	21	22	23
24	25	26	27	28	29	30
31						

JUNE

S	M	T	W	T	F	S
	1	2	3	4	5	6
7	8	9	10	11	12	13
14	15	16	17	18	19	20
21	22	23	24	25	26	27
28	29	30				

JULY

S	M	T	W	T	F	S
			1	2	3	4
5	6	7	8	9	10	11
12	13	14	15	16	17	18
19	20	21	22	23	24	25
26	27	28	29	30	31	

AUGUST

S	M	T	W	T	F	S
						1
2	3	4	5	6	7	8
9	10	11	12	13	14	15
16	17	18	19	20	21	22
23	24	25	26	27	28	29
30	31					

SEPTEMBER

S	M	T	W	T	F	S
		1	2	3	4	5
6	7	8	9	10	11	12
13	14	15	16	17	18	19
20	21	22	23	24	25	26
27	28	29	30			

OCTOBER

S	M	T	W	T	F	S
				1	2	3
4	5	6	7	8	9	10
11	12	13	14	15	16	17
18	19	20	21	22	23	24
25	26	27	28	29	30	31

NOVEMBER

S	M	T	W	T	F	S
1	2	3	4	5	6	7
8	9	10	11	12	13	14
15	16	17	18	19	20	21
22	23	24	25	26	27	28
29	30					

DECEMBER

S	M	T	W	T	F	S
		1	2	3	4	5
6	7	8	9	10	11	12
13	14	15	16	17	18	19
20	21	22	23	24	25	26
27	28	29	30	31		

1999

JANUARY

S	M	T	W	T	F	S
					1	2
3	4	5	6	7	8	9
10	11	12	13	14	15	16
17	18	19	20	21	22	23
24	25	26	27	28	29	30
31						

FEBRUARY

S	M	T	W	T	F	S
	1	2	3	4	5	6
7	8	9	10	11	12	13
14	15	16	17	18	19	20
21	22	23	24	25	26	27
28						

MARCH

S	M	T	W	T	F	S
	1	2	3	4	5	6
7	8	9	10	11	12	13
14	15	16	17	18	19	20
21	22	23	24	25	26	27
28	29	30	31			

APRIL

S	M	T	W	T	F	S
				1	2	3
4	5	6	7	8	9	10
11	12	13	14	15	16	17
18	19	20	21	22	23	24
25	26	27	28	29	30	

MAY

S	M	T	W	T	F	S
						1
2	3	4	5	6	7	8
9	10	11	12	13	14	15
16	17	18	19	20	21	22
23	24	25	26	27	28	29
30	31					

JUNE

S	M	T	W	T	F	S
		1	2	3	4	5
6	7	8	9	10	11	12
13	14	15	16	17	18	19
20	21	22	23	24	25	26
27	28	29	30			

JULY

S	M	T	W	T	F	S
				1	2	3
4	5	6	7	8	9	10
11	12	13	14	15	16	17
18	19	20	21	22	23	24
25	26	27	28	29	30	31

AUGUST

S	M	T	W	T	F	S
1	2	3	4	5	6	7
8	9	10	11	12	13	14
15	16	17	18	19	20	21
22	23	24	25	26	27	28
29	30	31				

SEPTEMBER

S	M	T	W	T	F	S
			1	2	3	4
5	6	7	8	9	10	11
12	13	14	15	16	17	18
19	20	21	22	23	24	25
26	27	28	29	30		

OCTOBER

S	M	T	W	T	F	S
					1	2
3	4	5	6	7	8	9
10	11	12	13	14	15	16
17	18	19	20	21	22	23
24	25	26	27	28	29	30
31						

NOVEMBER

S	M	T	W	T	F	S
	1	2	3	4	5	6
7	8	9	10	11	12	13
14	15	16	17	18	19	20
21	22	23	24	25	26	27
28	29	30				

DECEMBER

S	M	T	W	T	F	S
			1	2	3	4
5	6	7	8	9	10	11
12	13	14	15	16	17	18
19	20	21	22	23	24	25
26	27	28	29	30	31	

2000

JANUARY

S	M	T	W	T	F	S
						1
2	3	4	5	6	7	8
9	10	11	12	13	14	15
16	17	18	19	20	21	22
23	24	25	26	27	28	29
30	31					

FEBRUARY

S	M	T	W	T	F	S
		1	2	3	4	5
6	7	8	9	10	11	12
13	14	15	16	17	18	19
20	21	22	23	24	25	26
27	28	29				

MARCH

S	M	T	W	T	F	S
			1	2	3	4
5	6	7	8	9	10	11
12	13	14	15	16	17	18
19	20	21	22	23	24	25
26	27	28	29	30	31	

APRIL

S	M	T	W	T	F	S
						1
2	3	4	5	6	7	8
9	10	11	12	13	14	15
16	17	18	19	20	21	22
23	24	25	26	27	28	29
30						

MAY

S	M	T	W	T	F	S
	1	2	3	4	5	6
7	8	9	10	11	12	13
14	15	16	17	18	19	20
21	22	23	24	25	26	27
28	29	30	31			

JUNE

S	M	T	W	T	F	S
				1	2	3
4	5	6	7	8	9	10
11	12	13	14	15	16	17
18	19	20	21	22	23	24
25	26	27	28	29	30	

JULY

S	M	T	W	T	F	S
						1
2	3	4	5	6	7	8
9	10	11	12	13	14	15
16	17	18	19	20	21	22
23	24	25	26	27	28	29
30	31					

AUGUST

S	M	T	W	T	F	S
		1	2	3	4	5
6	7	8	9	10	11	12
13	14	15	16	17	18	19
20	21	22	23	24	25	26
27	28	29	30	31		

SEPTEMBER

S	M	T	W	T	F	S
					1	2
3	4	5	6	7	8	9
10	11	12	13	14	15	16
17	18	19	20	21	22	23
24	25	26	27	28	29	30

OCTOBER

S	M	T	W	T	F	S
1	2	3	4	5	6	7
8	9	10	11	12	13	14
15	16	17	18	19	20	21
22	23	24	25	26	27	28
29	30	31				

NOVEMBER

S	M	T	W	T	F	S
			1	2	3	4
5	6	7	8	9	10	11
12	13	14	15	16	17	18
19	20	21	22	23	24	25
26	27	28	29	30		

DECEMBER

S	M	T	W	T	F	S
					1	2
3	4	5	6	7	8	9
10	11	12	13	14	15	16
17	18	19	20	21	22	23
24	25	26	27	28	29	30
31						

2001

JANUARY

S	M	T	W	T	F	S
	1	2	3	4	5	6
7	8	9	10	11	12	13
14	15	16	17	18	19	20
21	22	23	24	25	26	27
28	29	30	31			

FEBRUARY

S	M	T	W	T	F	S
				1	2	3
4	5	6	7	8	9	10
11	12	13	14	15	16	17
18	19	20	21	22	23	24
25	26	27	28			

MARCH

S	M	T	W	T	F	S
				1	2	3
4	5	6	7	8	9	10
11	12	13	14	15	16	17
18	19	20	21	22	23	24
25	26	27	28	29	30	31

APRIL

S	M	T	W	T	F	S
1	2	3	4	5	6	7
8	9	10	11	12	13	14
15	16	17	18	19	20	21
22	23	24	25	26	27	28
29	30					

MAY

S	M	T	W	T	F	S
		1	2	3	4	5
6	7	8	9	10	11	12
13	14	15	16	17	18	19
20	21	22	23	24	25	26
27	28	29	30	31		

JUNE

S	M	T	W	T	F	S
					1	2
3	4	5	6	7	8	9
10	11	12	13	14	15	16
17	18	19	20	21	22	23
24	25	26	27	28	29	30

JULY

S	M	T	W	T	F	S
1	2	3	4	5	6	7
8	9	10	11	12	13	14
15	16	17	18	19	20	21
22	23	24	25	26	27	28
29	30	31				

AUGUST

S	M	T	W	T	F	S
			1	2	3	4
5	6	7	8	9	10	11
12	13	14	15	16	17	18
19	20	21	22	23	24	25
26	27	28	29	30	31	

SEPTEMBER

S	M	T	W	T	F	S
						1
2	3	4	5	6	7	8
9	10	11	12	13	14	15
16	17	18	19	20	21	22
23	24	25	26	27	28	29
30						

OCTOBER

S	M	T	W	T	F	S
	1	2	3	4	5	6
7	8	9	10	11	12	13
14	15	16	17	18	19	20
21	22	23	24	25	26	27
28	29	30	31			

NOVEMBER

S	M	T	W	T	F	S
				1	2	3
4	5	6	7	8	9	10
11	12	13	14	15	16	17
18	19	20	21	22	23	24
25	26	27	28	29	30	

DECEMBER

S	M	T	W	T	F	S
						1
2	3	4	5	6	7	8
9	10	11	12	13	14	15
16	17	18	19	20	21	22
23	24	25	26	27	28	29
30	31					